Toward a Linguistic Theory
of Speech Acts

Toward a Linguistic Theory of Speech Acts

JERROLD M. SADOCK

Department of Linguistics
University of Chicago
Chicago, Illinois

ACADEMIC PRESS *New York*   *San Francisco*   *London*

A Subsidiary of Harcourt Brace Jovanovich, Publishers

ACADEMIC PRESS, INC.
111 Fifth Avenue, New York, New York 10003

United Kingdom Edition published by
ACADEMIC PRESS, INC. (LONDON) LTD.
24/28 Oval Road, London NW1

Library of Congress Cataloging in Publication Data

Sadock, Jerrold M
    Toward a linguistic theory of speech acts.

    Bibliography: p.
    1.   Generative grammar.   I.   Title.
P151.S15   415   74-18405
ISBN 0-12-614350-1

To my parents

Contents

Preface

The study of speech acts has received a good deal of attention lately from philosophers and linguists, but no major work that represents contemporary linguistic thinking has previously appeared. This book is an attempt to fill that gap. It is almost entirely a linguistic work. I have tried to let the methodological rigor of generative grammar and the facts of natural languages, especially English, determine the outcome of the analysis.

Every language provides subtle and not-so-subtle means of encoding information about the intentions of the speaker and his assumptions about the speech situation in the sentences he uses. Using a conservative version of the theory of generative semantics, I show that the information of this kind that sentences can carry is considerably more detailed than had been thought.

On the one hand, I have used the theory of generative semantics to investigate speech acts, but, on the other, I have used the rich data that speech acts provide in order to test the theory of generative semantics. I have deliberately pushed the theory and refrained, as far as my will power allowed me, from speculating about sweeping innovations. This I did in order to be sure that I was working within a testable theory in the first place. One cannot dignify a set of beliefs with the title *theory* if that set of beliefs changes radically at the first hint of empirical trouble. The result of pushing the theory in this way has been the uncovering of certain very specific and serious sorts of difficulties. If the recognition of these problems leads a reader to new insights into the nature of language, even if these insights demolish the linguistic theory of speech acts that I present, I will feel that I have accomplished a great deal.

I have been thinking and writing about speech acts for more than seven years now and, although 1 continue to find new facts and to revise my ideas, I think I have learned something. In order to share with as wide an audience as possible what I have learned up to the summer of 1973, I have included quite a bit of background material including a sketch of generative semantics. I hope that philosophers and psychologists, in fact anyone interested in communication, will be able to use what I have written.

Acknowledgments

It is difficult to thank adequately all those whose efforts have contributed to this work, but I must especially mention the following:
Michael Geis, who urged me to pursue my interest in speech acts and
who taught me a great deal about syntax; Arnold Zwicky, whose
teaching also influenced me greatly, who tirelessly advised me during
the writing of the dissertation from which the present work ultimately
stems, and who read and made extremely helpful comments on a
preliminary version of the book; and James McCawley, Noriko
McCawley, and Ann Weiser, who also read and commented on portions of the manuscript.

I owe much also to those students and teachers who attended
seminars on speech acts which I gave at the University of Chicago
and The Ohio State University. I learned a great deal in these classes
and had a great deal of fun at the same time. I am grateful as well to
the participants in the workshop on formal pragmatics held in conjunction with the Summer Linguistic Institute at Ann Arbor in 1973.
They listened patiently to me and patiently corrected my thinking on
a number of points.

For typing and retyping the manuscript, I am deeply indebted to
Linda Matthews, Gail Sadock, Marlene Payha, and Betty Gau.

I wish also to apologize to those scholars whose relevant work is not
mentioned in this book. In a few cases, particularly T. Cohen (1973),
McCawley (forthcoming), and Vendler (1972), the work appeared too
late for inclusion. In the remaining cases, simple inadvertence or lack
of scholarship on my part is at fault.

1

Introduction

FORMAL LINGUISTICS

The goal of formal linguistics is to make explicit the relationship between linguistic meaning and linguistic form. Since native speakers of a language are capable of matching meaning and form both when they speak and when they apprehend speech, the formal description of this relationship for some language can be looked at as a model of the abstract linguistic competence of a speaker of that language. The formal system that makes explicit the mappings between meaning and form and vice versa is called a **grammar.** The grammar of a natural language can be conceived of as a device that specifies a set of all ordered pairs $< LS, SS >$, such that SS represents a grammatical sentence of the language and LS is a **logical structure** or **semantic representation** that represents a meaning of SS in the language.

There are infinitely many grammatical sentences within any language and an infinite number of expressible meanings. Hence, the number of ordered pairs $< LS, SS >$ is correspondingly infinite. One and the same sentence may express more than one meaning;

1

that is, two of the ordered pairs that comprise the language might be $< LS_i, SS_k >$ and $< LS_j, SS_k >$, where SS_k is a single surface structure and LS_i and LS_j are distinct logical structures. The existence of two such ordered pairs among those that comprise the language is a formal statement of the ambiguity of the surface structure SS_k. On the other hand, we might find also that the very same meaning is expressible in two ways. The formal statement of the synonymy of the distinct surface structures SS_j and SS_k would be the existence, among the ordered pairs that the grammar of the language specifies, of two ordered pairs, $< LS_i, SS_j >$ and $< LS_i, SS_k >$, where LS_i is a single logical form.

Nothing approaching an adequate grammar in this technical sense has been constructed for any natural language. Nevertheless, a good deal is known about the general characteristics that such a device is likely to have. In the first place, we have some idea of the form of the items LS and SS, the semantic representations and the surface representations, respectively.

The most superficial representation of a sentence would be a detailed description of its phonetic structures. In this book, however, I will deal only with the relationship that exists between meaning and the arrangement of morphemes; that is, I will deal only with syntax. Thus, I assume that there is an autonomous component of the grammar—the phonological component—that is responsible for specifying the mappings between surface syntactic structure and phonetic structure.[1]

The assumption of autonomous syntactic and phonological components forces certain requirements on the surface syntactic representations. Besides specifying the left-to-right order of morphemes, which it obviously must do, the surface syntactic representation must include other sorts of information. Notice that the stress of the words *record* (verb) and *record* (noun) differ. Yet they both consist of the same two morphemes in the same order. The surface syntactic representation must therefore specify the syntactic category to which groups of morphemes belong, for otherwise it would be impossible for an autonomous phonological component to correctly specify the placement of stress within words. Note also that the string of words *Job cursed the day he was born* (Jespersen, 1963: 103n) can have two different pronunciations, each of which is associated with a different

---

[1] This assumption has been at least partially called into question by Bresnan (1971). I shall deal mainly with high-level syntactic processes and with logical structure itself and it therefore does not seem to me that a great deal rides on the correctness of the assumption that phonology and syntax are autonomous.

sense of the sentence. With the meaning "Job used profanity early in life," there can be a pause between *cursed* and *the*, and heavier stress on *cursed* than on *day*. When the string means "Job lamented having been born," there can be no pause between *cursed* and *the*, and the heavier stress may fall on *day* rather than on *cursed*. This difference in intonation is clearly related to the fact that in the latter sentence, *cursed the day he was born* is a unit, or a **constituent,** of the sentence, while in the former case, it is not. Because of facts like this, it is necessary for the surface syntactic representation to include information as to how morphemes are grouped together into constituents and how these constituents are, in turn, grouped into larger constituents.

All this information can be conveniently set forth in a labeled branching diagram, or **tree.** For the sentence just presented, in the sense it has in the Bible, a reasonably good approximation of a surface-structure tree would be the following:

(1)

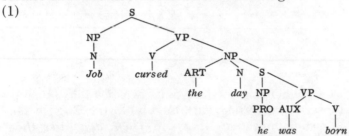

The labels S, NP, N, V, ART, PRO, and AUX have the formal function of indicating what stretches of material belong to what categories. Thus, *Job* and *the day he was born* are constituents that belong to the same category, the category called "NP." The specific labels for the various kinds of surface syntactic constituents are mnemonically chosen: S for sentence, NP for noun phrase, N for noun, VP for verb phrase, V for verb, ART for article, PRO for pronoun, and AUX for auxiliary. There is no particular theoretical importance attached to the choice of these labels.

There are certain minimal requirements on semantic representations as well. For example, the difference in sense between the sentences *My keeshond bit the postman* and *The postman bit my keeshond* must be reflected in an adequate system of semantic representation. It would appear to be the order of elements which is involved in this meaning difference, and, hence, it would seem that elements must appear in a specified order in semantic representation.

Semantic representations must also be able to display the two different senses that a sentence like *All linguists don't speak Sogdian* can have, depending on whether or not *all* receives special high stress. The difference in this case involves the hierarchical relationship among the various elements. In one case, it is asserted that for all linguists it is the case that they do not speak Sogdian; in the other, it is asserted that it is not true that all linguists speak Sogdian.

Labeled trees such as those used to represent surface structures include both the ordering and the hierarchical information that appear to be necessary in an adequate semantic theory. Unfortunately, it is clear that this sort of labeled tree contains too much information. To see this, consider the possible arrangements of the elements (assuming for the moment that they are semantic elements, which is without a doubt untrue) *postman, bite, dog*. These can be put into a minimal semantic tree in six ways:

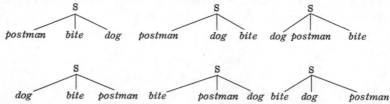

But these three elements enter into only two possible semantic relationships, those which correspond (roughly) to the English sentences *The/a postman bites the/a dog* and *The/a dog bites the/a postman*. Very little work has been done with an eye toward sharpening semantic theory to the point where its representations include **only** semantically relevant information while, of course, including all that is needed. Neither is it the point of this book to institute such a revision. Consequently, I will assume throughout this work that semantic representations are in the form of labeled trees.

As to the form of the syntactic component—the formal device whose job it is to specify the mapping between the labeled trees that represent meaning and those that represent surface syntactic form—there are at present two rather different general proposals. I will describe only the theory employed in this book. Although I am convinced of its essential correctness, I will not attempt to justify this formalism here but will instead refer the reader to Lakoff (1970d), McCawley (to appear), Postal (1970), and Ross (1969b).

The model of grammar that has been adopted for the purposes of this book is somewhat misleadingly referred to as **generative semantics.** It proposes that semantic trees are modified in a long series of steps until they are transmuted into surface syntactic trees. An allowable series of modifications from semantic to surface structure is called a **derivation.** Whether or not some sequence of steps LS, P_1, $P_2, \ldots, P_{n-1}, P_n$, SS is a derivation, and, hence, whether the ordered pair $< $ LS, SS $ >$ is part of the language specified by the grammar, is determined by the rules of the grammar.

These rules are of two types. First, there are **transformations,** which specify how two adjacent steps in a derivation may differ. For example, a well-supported transformational rule, generally called "Equi–NP deletion," "Equi," or "END," provides, among other things, that if P_k, some intermediate stage of derivation, contains the substructure

(2)

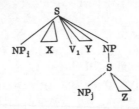

and NP_i and NP_j refer to the same entity, and if V_1 is a verb of a certain class, then P_{k+1}, the succeeding stage in the derivation, may have subtree (3) in place of subtree (2):

(3)

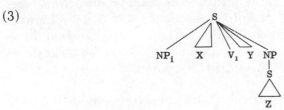

This rule allows the deletion of the subject of a dependent clause if it is coreferent with the subject of an immediately higher clause containing a verb of a specified class. It accounts for the fact that, in a sentence such as *Nansen wished to reach the Pole,* we understand the semantic subject of the verb *reach* to be Nansen. In the semantic representation of this sentence, a noun phrase that refers to Nansen will, in fact, be the subject of *reach.* But during the derivation from logical to surface structure, this noun phrase is deleted as allowed by the transformational rule of Equi–NP deletion just described. That is, the derivation of the sentence includes successive tree structures that contain subtrees of the forms (2) and (3), in that order.

Most transformational rules apply to trees **cyclically.** That is, they apply as a group first to the most deeply embedded clauses, then to the next most deeply embedded clauses, and so on to the top of the tree. It is generally believed that within the cycle, the transformational rules are **extrinsically linearly ordered.** That is, in applying to each clause, the transformations apply in a specified order.

In addition to the cyclic transformations, it is quite likely that there must also be a block of **postcyclic rules** that apply to the entire tree at only one point in the derivation, possibly in several places simultaneously, in an externally specified order and after the last of the cyclic rules has applied to the highest clause.

It has been demonstrated recently (Partee, 1970, and G. Lakoff, 1970b) that a grammar whose only mechanism for deriving surface structures from semantic structures is a set of transformational rules is not adequate to the task of specifying all, and only, the pairings of semantic representations and surface syntactic representations that characterize natural languages. The problem is that transformational rules cannot see further back in derivations than the input tree. It turns out that earlier derivational history is sometimes relevant to the operation of a rule. Of course, it is always possible to write special ad hoc rules that mark structures as having certain properties, and then to carry these markers past the point where the properties in question have ceased to exist.[2] Subsequent transformations could then be made sensitive to the presence or absence of such markers and, therefore, to earlier structural information that is not otherwise present in the tree to which the rules apply. This strategem, however, amounts to the claim that grammars of natural languages contain processes that are not myopic in the sense that classical transformations are.

A more powerful sort of device that has been proposed to answer the deficiencies of classical transformations is the **derivational constraint.** Properly speaking, transformations are a particular sort of derivational constraint,[3] but there are some derivational constraints of essentially greater power than transformations.

Among the rules of the grammar are those that insert lexical items and multiword idioms. Semantic representations do not contain lexical items but, rather, semantically primitive elements. It is far from clear, at present, what the inventory of semantic primes is for any na-

---

[2] Baker and Brame (1972) propose that such markers be used to encode derivational history in trees.

[3] This view of transformations is due to G. Lakoff (see, for example, G. Lakoff, 1970d).

tural language, and whether there is a universal set of such atomic elements or whether the set differs from language to language. At any rate, since surface structures contain lexical items, these must be inserted at some stage of derivation. As an illustration of a rule of lexical insertion, consider the distribution of a so-called "negative-polarity item" such as the phrase *a red cent*. There are two basic principles governing its distribution. First, it can occur only in a clause that is **semantically** negated, as the following paradigm shows:

(4)   *John has a red cent.*
(5)   *John doesn't have a red cent.*
(6)   *John didn't manage to have a red cent.*
(7)   *John failed to save a red cent.*
(8)   *John didn't fail to save a red cent.*

Second, this phrase must follow the negative element in surface structure:

(9)   *John didn't save a red cent.*
(10)   *A red cent wasn't saved by John.*
(11)   *Not a red cent was saved by John.*

Thus, the insertion of this negative-polarity item must be governed by a derivational constraint. It must take place at a late enough stage of derivation to ensure that it follows the negative element in surface structure, but it must be sensitive to semantic information concerning negation that may become lost—as in (7) and (8)—in the course of the derivation.

In addition to grammatical rules which define the steps in a derivation, there are constraints on the form of the structures at the end points of derivations. There are independent rules of semantic well-formedness and independent rules of surface-structure well-formedness (often called **output constraints** cf. Perlmutter, 1972). The existence of constraints of the former kind ought to be fairly obvious. They guarantee the coherence of semantic representations and ensure that information that is required, perhaps language specifically, is present. For example, some languages require that every assertion be accompanied by an indication of the speaker's authority for making the assertion. English does not place this requirement on semantic structures but does impose others that are lacking in other languages. For example, any sentence of English that requires the use of a third-person singular pronoun that refers to a human being must mention the sex of the referent. We cannot avoid making known the sex of the person referred to by the phrase *my neighbor* in a sentence such as

(12)   *My neighbor shook her head.*

But other languages (e.g., Eskimo) make no such demands on semantic representations. Our language demands that notions expressed by active verbs be accompanied by an indication of whether the action described is viewed as ongoing or completed, whereas this information is optional in the better-known European languages.

Danish gives us a straightforward example of an output constraint. In Danish, no two consecutive surface clauses can begin with the word *som*, although this phonological form has two entirely different semantic and syntactic sources. It is either a relative particle like English *that* or a subordinating conjunction with approximately the sense of English *as*. For a detailed description of this constraint, see Sadock (1972a).

Within the conception of grammar that I shall adopt in this book, then, the pairings of semantic structures with surface structures that characterize a language are the end points of those derivations that survive the rigors of transformational rules, derivational constraints, rules of semantic well-formedness, and output constraints.

SPEECH ACTS

In his famous William James lectures (Austin, 1965), the philosopher John Austin recognized and described a fundamental trichotomy among the things we do when we use language. According to Austin, linguistic acts fall into three categories, which he called "locutionary," "perlocutionary," and "illocutionary" acts.

Locutionary acts are acts that are performed in order to communicate. In speaking, acts of phonation (e.g., aspirating a /t/, closing the glottis, producing a second formant with a frequency of 2700Hz, etc.) belong in this class. There are analogous acts that are performed in the process of nonvocal communication acts, like dotting an *i* or holding down a telegraph key for one-tenth of a second. Higher-order grammatical acts also belong in this category. Using the word *axolotl*, ending a sentence with a preposition, predicating the baldness of the King of France, and referring to Pegasus are all locutionary acts. This book will not deal further with locutionary acts, since their study is the domain of fields like phonetics, phonology, syntax, and linguistic semantics.

Perlocutionary acts are the by-products of acts of communication. By uttering the sentence *You don't look a day over forty*, one might flatter an elderly person to whom it was addressed, amuse or insult a young addressee, embarrass oneself, and so on. The perlocutionary effect of an utterance may be intentional or unintentional. It is characteristic of utterances that they have numerous perlocutionary effects, and it is also characteristic that the number of intended perlocutionary effects associated with an utterance is not limited. We may always deny that a particular perlocutionary act was intended by saying things like *I didn't mean to embarrass you* or *I was simply stating a fact.*

Illocutionary acts are speech acts that we accomplish by communicating our intent to accomplish them. An illocutionary act is the conventional force of an utterance. There are numerous ways in which our intended illocution can be communicated. The most straightforward is to mention directly what we are doing in making a particular utterance, as when we say *I pronounce the defendant guilty, I promise you that I'll mend the spinnaker,* and so on. An utterance of this form, whose highest clause has a first-person singular subject and a verb in the simple present that conveys the intended force of the utterance, is called an **explicit performative,** or sometimes just a **performative.**

Performative utterances were first investigated by philosophers because, while they resemble declarative sentences in form, they are not subject to judgments of truth and falsity. While a statement like *Bill bets on the Mets* can be adjudged true or false depending on the circumstances, the sentence *I hereby bet on the Mets* is neither true nor false. It may succeed or fail as a bet—for example, it may not be heard or it may not be taken up—but this is quite different from its being false. If the illocutionary force of a sentence takes effect, the utterance is said to be **happy** or **felicitous.** If it goes awry for some reason, it is **unhappy** or **infelicitous.** The factors that determine whether a particular illocutionary act succeeds are termed **felicity conditions.** For example, a bet cannot take place unless both parties agree to it. A redoubling in bridge cannot take place unless someone has doubled, and an announcement cannot succeed in informing if the addressee was already aware of the content of the announcement.

It can now be seen that while the propositional content of a declarative sentence can be true or false, the sentence itself, since it is an illocutionary act of assertion, is not true or false but felicitous or infelicitous.

In the majority of cases, the illocutionary force of an utterance is not signaled by a performative formula. Natural languages employ several more subtle means of indicating what the speaker is doing in saying something. The illocutionary act of inquiring, for example, can sometimes be accomplished through the use of an explicit performative, as when a lawyer says to a witness *I ask you whether you poisoned Fred Smurd.* Normally, however, the fact that a particular utterance is a question is signaled by one or more of the following devices in various natural languages.

Word order: English verb-first word order is often the sign of an act of inquiring, as in *Is it snowing?*

Intonation: Yes–no questions in Modern Hebrew (and numerous other languages) can be signaled just by a special intonation pattern.

Special morphemes: In Yiddish, questions that require a yes-or-no answer are introduced by an interrogative particle. In Eskimo, special personal endings on verbs indicate a question. The interrogative morpheme found in such words as *which, where,* and *what* in English is also an example of this type.

Deletion: Test questions in English can sometimes be signaled by deletion of the questioned element. An example is *The first person to cross the Greenland icecap was _____?* Deletion of a second-person subject is a frequent marker of requests or orders in a variety of languages.

Very often more than one of these nonperformative signals combine to indicate the illocutionary force of a sentence. This is, in fact, the case with most of the examples just given. A Yiddish yes–no question is not only marked with the interrogative particle but also has inverted word order and a special sentence-final intonation contour.

(13)   *Er hot gegesn a halbn xazer.*
                he has eaten a half pig
                ("He ate half a pig.")
(14)   *Ci hot er gegesn a halbn xazer?*
                Int. has he eaten a half pig
                ("Did he eat half a pig?")

The illocutionary force of an utterance is always interpreted as having been intended. For this reason, it is ordinarily impossible to deny that it was one's intention to perform an illocutionary act that one has performed (but see page 11). If one says *I christen this ship "The Kneydel"* while breaking a bottle of champagne on the stem of a vessel, it would raise more than a few eyebrows to say

subsequently, *I'm sorry. I didn't mean to christen this ship.*
Similarly, if one says to his Intourist guide *Where are your offensive missiles located?* it would do little good to protest to the authorities later that he was stating a fact. To claim that one was not responsible for one's own illocutionary act is to claim that one was not **responsible** at the time of the utterance.

Generally speaking, it is the case that there is associated with a single sentence one and only one illocutionary force. There are, however, some fairly obvious sorts of exceptions to this observation. First of all, a single sentence can be a conjunction of two or more clauses, each of which can have its own illocutionary force—for example, *I promise to brush my teeth after eating saganaki and I demand that you do the same.* A sentence can also be ambiguous as to illocutionary force. A single instance of the use of such a sentence will still have only one intended illocutionary force; but on another occasion, the uttering of the same string of words could have quite a different force. For example, sentences that follow the explicit performative formula are usually ambiguous between a performative sense and a constative (assertive) sense. An occurrence of the sentence *I bet the administration will embarrass itself* can on one occasion be an illocutionary act of betting. But as an answer to the question *How do you make so much money?* it is not a bet, but something more like an assertion. The third apparent counterexample to the principle that each utterance has one illocutionary force involves the entailment of illocutionary force. As has often been observed, requesting that someone tell you something entails asking it. It is not immediately clear in such cases, however, whether the entailed force is illocutionary or perlocutionary, but more will be said about this problem in Chapter 5.

When a sentence is uttered that is ambiguous as to illocutionary force, it is also possible to disavow responsibility for one or the other of the illocutionary forces that the sentence can have. An instance of this is illustrated by the following dialogue:

(15)   A: *How do you make so much money?*
          B: *I bet the administration will embarrass itself.*
          A: *You're on!*
          B: *That wasn't a bet. I was just telling you
          how I make my money.*

This case looks very similar to cases of the disavowal of a perlocutionary intent. In fact, there is still a difference. Here B is denying that he did what A thought he did, and not just saying that he intended to do something other than what he actually accomplished. In a way, B is claiming that he didn't **say** what A thought he said, but uttered a different sentence that happened to sound the same.

Illocutionary acts are basic to our communicative ability. Using language involves more than simply stringing out and stacking up abstract propositions. For communication to take place, we must also indicate what it is we are doing with these propositions, and we must also be able to apprehend the pragmatic significance of the utterances of others. This book aims at establishing and examining a theory of illocutionary acts within the framework of the semantically based grammar outlined in this chapter—that is, to give a formal account of this fundamental aspect of communication. In order to do so, it will be necessary to provide a means of distinguishing illocutionary from perlocutionary force in other than the intuitive manner that was used here. This will be done in Chapter 5.

FORMAL LINGUISTICS AND ILLOCUTIONARY ACTS

No theory of grammar can completely avoid treating illocutionary force because of the existence of explicit performatives. The surface form of such sentences is a good first approximation of the meaning of the sentence, including its pragmatic significance. But what of sentences whose illocutionary force is reflected by one or more of the indirect means mentioned in the preceding discussion?

The earliest transformational grammars, for example the sketch given by Chomsky (1957), included optionally applicable transformations that accounted for the surface form of the various speech-act types. The declarative form was considered to reflect underlying syntactic structure, and two optional transformations were supplied—one that permuted the positions of the subject and the tense morpheme, and another that deleted a second-person subject. These transformations affected illocutionary force. Some undiscussed interpretive device would have been required to pair exactly the structures to which the inversion transformation had applied with logical structures representative of interrogative force, and those to which the subject-deletion rule had applied with logical structures that represent the appropriate request sense. The rules of semantic interpretation would have to operate after or in conjunction with the application of the optional sentence-type transformations, but these semantic rules were never discussed in detail.

The next modification of linguistic theory that is pertinent to the present discussion was introduced by Katz and Postal (1964). These authors wished to eliminate all meaning-changing transformations. A good part of the motivation for this was the fact that the majority of transformational rules that had been suggested up to that time were, indeed, meaning-preserving. Two of the most striking exceptions were the interrogative and imperative transformations. To eliminate the meaning-changing property of these rules, it was necessary for Katz and Postal to argue that there existed some difference in the syntactic structures that underlie declarative, imperative, and interrogative sentences. Then rules that matched semantic structures with syntactic ones could make use of the underlying difference between the various sentence types and would not need to take into account the application or lack of application of the sentence-type transformations. The underlying structural difference between questions,

(16)

Level	Structure	Rules
Deep syntactic		Formed by phase-structure rules
Intermediate stages of derivation		A: Imperative transformation B: Question transformation C: Other transformation
Surface syntactic		
		Undescribed semantic rules
Semantic	Imperative (undescribed) Question (undescribed) Assertion (undescribed)	

(17)

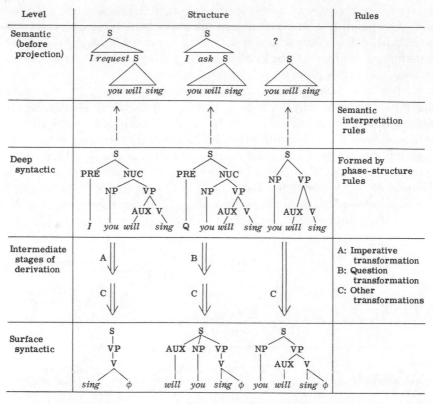

Level	Structure			Rules
Semantic (before projection)	S / I request S / you will sing	S / I ask S / you will sing	? S / you will sing	
	↑	↑	↑	Semantic interpretation rules
Deep syntactic	S / PRE NUC / NP VP / AUX V / I you will sing	S / PRE NUC / NP VP / AUX V / Q you will sing	S / NP VP / AUX V / you will sing	Formed by phase-structure rules
Intermediate stages of derivation	A ⇓ C ⇓	B ⇓ C ⇓	⇓ C ⇓	A: Imperative transformation B: Question transformation C: Other transformations
Surface syntactic	S / VP / V / sing φ	S / AUX NP VP / V / will you sing φ	S / NP VP / AUX V / you will sing φ	

requests, and assertions that Katz and Postal suggested was the presence of the ad hoc presentential markers Q (for questions) and I (for requests). Assertions were not provided with a presentential marker. Katz and Postal also assumed that imperatives contain the modal *will* at the deep syntactic level. They described the semantic significance of the interrogative and imperative markers as being similar to a higher performative clause, although they didn't describe the required semantic interpretation rule further. These two early transformational treatments of the major sentence types are contrasted diagramatically in (16), representing Chomsky's earlier theory, and (17), which portrays Katz and Postal's.

In several respects, Katz and Postal's scheme is an improvement over Chomsky's. It retains the advantages of claiming that there is a transformational relationship among the three sentence types, since, as can be seen in diagram (17), sentences that differ only in sentence type contain the same subtree, NUC, the "nucleus" of the sentence, in underlying representation. With this shared constituent, one need not state several times the semantic restrictions that are shared by all three sentence types. The fact that all three of the sentences, *You will elapse, *Will you elapse?, and *Elapse., are anomalous in the same way can be traced uniformly to the same anomalous underlying constituent. Moreover, the underlying illocutionary-force markers can be used to explain the fact that the sentence You will close the door is apparently ambiguous between a reading with assertive force and one with the force of an order. All that need be done is to assume that the imperative transformation applies optionally in the presence of the imperative markers. Thus, two distinct underlying structures, one containing the imperative marker and one lacking it, would underlie the same surface structure and account for its ambiguity.

Some additional evidence that can be used in support of Katz and Postal's treatment, as opposed to Chomsky's, involves sentence adverbs. As the following paradigm shows, these occur freely only with declarative sentences:

(18)   *Fortunately, Hilda hid the evidence.*
(19)   **Fortunately, did Hilda hide the evidence?*
(20)   **Fortunately, hide the evidence.*

Lees (1965) pointed out that this fact can be neatly accounted for by making the symbol SADV (sentence adverb) an alternative expansion of the node that dominates the interrogative and imperative markers. He suggested a phrase-structure rule of the form PRE → {I, Q, SADV} to accommodate the fact that these three items are mutually exclusive in their occurrence. This also accounts for the fact that with sentence adverbs, only an assertive reading is available for a sentence like *Fortunately, you will hide the evidence.*

The presence of *will* in the underlying structure of imperatives allows the prediction of the correct range of time adverbials on the same basis as that used for specifying possible time adverbials in other sentence types. We find the following paradigm, for example, which is explained by the assumption of an underlying *will* in imperatives.

(21) $Defend\ my\ honor \left\{ \begin{array}{l} tomorrow \\ *yesterday \\ now \end{array} \right\}.$

(22) $Arturo\ will\ defend\ my\ honor \left\{ \begin{array}{l} tomorrow \\ *yesterday \\ now \end{array} \right\}.$

(23)   *Who will defend my honor* $\begin{Bmatrix} tomorrow \\ *yesterday \\ now \end{Bmatrix}$?

Katz and Postal also brought up the so-called "tag imperative" as evidence supporting the postulation of an underlying *will* in imperatives. Sentences such as *Thaw dinner, will you?* were taken as analogous to tag questions, such as *The plural of proboscis is proboscides, isn't it?* In tag questions, the tag contains a copy of the auxiliary in the base part of the sentence:

(24)   *Pigs can swim,* $\begin{Bmatrix} can't \\ *won't \\ *don't \end{Bmatrix}$ *they?*

Thus, the existence of *will* in the tag of tag imperatives would seem to give evidence of an underlying *will* in the base. This argument is, however, almost entirely vitiated by the existence of other modals in tag imperatives:

(25)   *Decant the Beaune,* $\begin{Bmatrix} will\ you \\ could\ you \\ why\ don't\ you \end{Bmatrix}$?

For further evidence that casts doubt on this argument for *will*, see Bolinger (1967). Much closer scrutiny will be given to tag questions and tag imperatives in Chapters 5 and 6.

Within a semantically based grammar, the underlying syntactic representation (i.e., the logical representation) of a sentence whose illocutionary force is not directly represented in surface structure in terms of a performative formula will still have to contain the semantic correspondent of a higher performative clause defining the illocutionary force of the sentence. This **abstract-performative hypothesis** was first investigated by Ross and presented later in print in his article "On Declarative Sentences" (Ross, 1970). This idea is, in fact, a rather old one. Katz and Postal (1964) suggested deriving interrogative and imperative sentences from structures that resemble explicitly performative structures, but, as we have seen, did not adopt this suggestion. Outside of transformational grammar, many tantalizingly similar notions can be found. In his German grammar, Whitney (1870:205) writes,

> When, now, we come to speak in our own persons, we change *ich behaupte, dass du mich liebst,* "I maintain that thou lovest me," into *du liebst mich,* "thou lovest me," the assertion of the assertion being usually a quite unnecessary formality; *ich will wissen, ob du mich liebest,* "I wish to know whether thou lovest me," becomes *liebst du mich,* "lovest thou me?" the wish to know being intimated by arrangement and tone; and *ich verlange, dass du*

mich liebest, "I require that thou love me," is changed into *liebe du mich,*
"love thou me!" the desire or demand being expressed by arrangement, tone,
and appropriate verbal form.

Even older allusions to the same idea can be found, for example in
Lane (1700).

In its simplest form, the abstract-performative hypothesis provides
that every sentence contain as its highest deep-syntactic (and semantic) clause a structure like those that give rise to explicit performatives. This contains a subject that refers to the speaker, an abstract
performative verb that specifies the force of the sentence, an indirect
object that refers to the addressee, and a clausal direct object. In the
case of explicitly performative sentences, no drastic changes affect
the performative clause during the syntactic derivation. In the case
of utterances that are not explicitly performative, the highest clause
is eventually deleted. A good part of the remainder of this book will
be devoted to exploring the problems that the abstract-performative
analysis entails, and to refining the proposal on the basis of these in-
vestigations.

The treatment of the major sentence types under the first-approx-
imation, generative-semantic approach is given schematically in (26)
(see page 18). Here, and in the remainder of the book, terminal nodes
in uppercase letters represent abstract lexical items , the symbol $\overset{NP}{\underset{I}{|}}$
represents a noun phrase that refers to the speaker, and the sym-
bol $\overset{NP}{\underset{You}{|}}$ indicates a noun phrase that refers to the addressee.

This treatment can be seen not only to **account** for some of the
facts that Katz and Postal's theory accounted for, but also to **explain**
them. The fact that a single sentence has only a single illocutionary
force follows naturally from the fact that there can be only one
highest surface clause. In Katz and Postal's theory, this fact was accommodated by the **assumption** that the illocutionary force markers
are alternative expansions of the same symbol, which is not the only
a priori possibility. Under the abstract-performative hypothesis, on
the other hand, the singularity of illocutionary force is predicted on
the basis of general and independently needed postulates concerning constructional possibilities. The theory of abstract performatives also explains why only the highest surface clause has an associated illocutionary force. While further ad hoc assumptions must
be added to Katz and Postal's list of assumptions in order to bring the
theory into line with this empirical observation, the fact is that no
modification of the abstract-performative theory is needed to account
for this fact.

(26)

Level	Structure	Rules
Semantic	[Tree 1] S → NP (I) VP (DECLARE) NP (You) S → NP (You) VP (will) VP (sing) — "You will sing" [Tree 2] S → NP (I) VP (ASK) NP (You) S → NP (You) VP (will) VP (sing) — "You will sing" [Tree 3] S → NP (I) VP (REQUEST) NP (You) S → NP (You) VP (will) VP (sing) — "You will sing"	Must meet criteria of semantic well-formedness
Intermediate stages of derivation	Tree 1: C ⇒ D ⇒ Tree 2: A ⇒ C ⇒ D ⇒ Tree 3: B ⇒ C ⇒ D ⇒	A: Question transformation B: Imperative transformation C: Performative deletion D: Other transformations
Surface syntactic	Tree 1: S → NP (You will) VP → V (sing) φ Tree 2: S → V (Will) NP (you) VP → V (sing) φ Tree 3: S → VP → V (sing) φ	Must meet output conditions

It is also possible to explain, rather than simply observe, the facts concerning the distribution of sentence adverbs by adopting the abstract-performative hypothesis. The demonstration of this involves a knowledge of a number of details of the behavior of adverbs in general and will be given in the next chapter, along with additional arguments in favor of the abstract-performative hypothesis.

The theory of abstract performatives, then, entails the following assumptions:

1. There exist constraints on the well-formedness of semantic representations to the effect that in the highest semantic proposition, (a) the subject refers to the speaker of the sentence; (b) the indirect object refers to the addressee; and (c) the verb is a performative verb of linguistic communication.

2. There is a rule (or set of rules) that deletes the highest semantic clause at some stage of derivation under certain circumstances.

The precise domain of application of the rule referred to is an extremely interesting and important question in the linguistic study of speech acts. This question will be examined in Chapter 6.

Note that the abstract-performative hypothesis explicitly makes the claim that illocutionary force is part of the meaning of sentences. Therefore, the linguistic theory agrees entirely with L. J. Cohen's (1971) stance. All aspects of the meaning of an utterance are locutionary acts, and illocutionary force is therefore a variety of locutionary act. It is now possible, however, to circumscribe exactly that portion of the meaning of sentences which defines their illocutionary force in a general way that was not available to Cohen. Whereas Cohen was forced to describe illocutionary force in a disjunction (L. J. Cohen, 1971:587)—

> The illocutionary force of an utterance is that aspect of its meaning which is either conveyed by its explicitly performative formula, if it has one, or might have been so conveyed by the use of such an expression—

it is possible within the framework of the abstract-performative theory to pin down illocutionary force in a unified way. We may say that **illocutionary force is that part of the meaning of a sentence which corresponds to the highest clause in its semantic representation.**

The ability of this theory to produce such generalizations is the strongest argument for its adoption. Numerous additional generalizations, both semantic and syntactic, will be shown in the next chapter to be attainable through the adoption of the abstract-performative-clause proposal.

2

The Evidence for the Performative Analysis

PRONOMINALIZATION AND RELATED PHENOMENA

In the years since Ross suggested the possible merits of the performative analysis of nonovert performatives, numerous linguists have contributed evidence in support of it. Relevant works include R. Lakoff (1968), McCawley (1968), Ross (1969c and 1970), Sadock (1969a and 1969b), Harada (1970), Lee and Maxwell (1970), and Schreiber (1972). In this chapter, I wish to outline a number of what seem to me to be the strongest of these arguments. For additional arguments, consult the works just referred to.

The greater number of syntactic arguments that have been offered in support of higher abstract performative clauses are of a single form: First, it is shown that some particular property of embedded sentences is directly traceable to some property or properties of the matrix sentence. Next, it is shown that the facts that held for embedded sentences also characterize certain highest surface clauses. One therefore concludes that a higher matrix structure with the appropriate structural properties is present at the stage of derivation at which the property of the embedded sentence is determined. The following argument from Ross (1970) is one of the most straightforward of this type.

Ordinarily, reflexive pronouns occur in grammatical sentences only if there is a coreferent antecedent in the same clause:

(1)   *Mary said that Bill promoted himself.*
(2)   **Bill said that Mary promoted himself.*

There are, however, numerous sorts of "spurious" reflexives whose antecedent need not be in the same clause. One instance of these is found in the object of the preposition *like* in reduced relative clauses:

(3)   *Fritz$_i$ knows that politicians like himself$_i$ are outmoded.*

(Here, and in the remainder of this book, identical subscripts on noun phrases indicate coreference.)

Notice, though, that for this spurious third-person reflexive to occur grammatically in a subordinate clause, there must be an antecedent elsewhere in the sentence:

(4)   **The democrats$_i$ know that politicians like himself$_i$ are outmoded.*

The antecedent can be in any higher clause, but not in a lower clause:

(5)   *The prince$_i$ told his footman that he should tell the people that nobles like himself$_i$ never bathe.*
(6)   *That a man like himself$_i$ could become rich didn't surprise Grosvenor$_i$.*
(7)   **A man like himself$_i$ wanted Carl$_i$ to run for Grand Dragon.*

The antecedent can be the subject, direct object, or indirect object of the clause in which it is found, as examples (3), (6), and (8) show. There is, however, some dialect variation on the last point; this is indicated by the superscript *d* in example (8).

(8)   *^{d}I told Peter$_i$ and Phil$_j$ that people like themselves$_{ij}$ shouldn't study Cabalah.*

Now, spurious first- and second-person reflexives after *like* occur freely, whether there is an overt antecedent or not. Note that there is some dialect variation with regard to second-person reflexives:

(9)   *Linguists like myself speak an even number of languages*

(10)   *ªThat a man like yourself would resort to such tactics disturbs me greatly.*

Both cases, that of spurious third-person reflexives with coreferent antecedents in a higher clause and that of first- and second-person reflexives with no surface antecedent, can be explained in the same way under the higher-performative-clause analysis. Let us suppose that the rule that produces spurious reflexives is a transformational rule that performs the following tree changes:

(11)

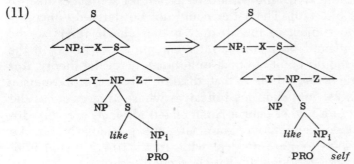

(Here, X, Y, and Z are variables that can include sentence nodes.) It is quite likely that this formulation is incorrect in several respects; but that fact is irrelevant to the present argument, since whatever the correct formulation might be, it would have the general effect of the simple-minded rule just given. Rule (11), or its equivalent, accounts for the facts of first and second-person reflexives automatically when combined with the abstract-performative hypothesis. By assumption, the structure of a sentence like (9) would, at some stage of derivation, be roughly like (12)

(12)

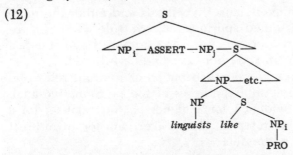

where the noun phrases labeled NP_i are coreferent and refer to the speaker of the sentence. The independently needed rule (11) can apply to structure (12) to produce the spurious reflexive. Subsequently, the performative clause will be deleted, yielding sentence (9).

Now let us consider the dialect variation mentioned earlier to determine whether or not an indirect object in a higher clause can function as the antecedent for this process. Recall that there is also dialect variation regarding whether second-person reflexives after *like* can occur freely without an overt antecedent in a higher clause. These facts could also be elegantly explained under the higher-clause analysis. A more restricted rule than (12), one that provided that only subjects of higher clauses could serve as the antecedent in this kind of reflexivization, would yield neither sentences like (8) nor sentences like (10). The latter could not be derived, since, by hypothesis, the subject of the abstract higher clause refers to the speaker, and all and only coreferent noun phrases will be in the first person. I should point out that, unfortunately for the theory, it is not always the same idiolect that disallows both second-person spurious reflexives and spurious reflexives whose antecedent is the indirect object of a higher clause. Such mixed idiolects are very difficult for orthodox generative grammar, and particularly for the theory under scrutiny here, to deal with. In treating a mixed idiolect—say, the attested one in which second-person spurious reflexives after *like* are found, but in which indirect objects of higher overt clauses cannot function as the antecedent for spurious reflexivization—no generalization between the two cases can be drawn. I suggest, however, that the problem is a diachronic, not a synchronic, one. The presently existing idiolects may not be regular when viewed individually, but the sequence of events that brought them to their present state must make historical sense. A reasonable starting point for the development of the present mixed dialects would be one in which the two "pure" dialects coexisted—those that are predicted by the abstract-higher-clause hypothesis and either the more general or the more restricted spurious-reflexive rule. Children exposed to both dialects would then have had primary linguistic data available from which the mixed idiolects could be inferred.

Returning to the main topic, the distribution of spurious reflexives after *like* supports several subhypotheses of the performative analysis. These facts give evidence for a higher abstract clause, for a subject of that clause that refers to the speaker, and for an indirect object that refers to the addressee.

There are several other spurious reflexives that are distributed in very similar ways. Third-person reflexives in these cases require an antecedent, while first- or second-person reflexives do not. Whatever further structural facts are necessary for a third-person noun phrase to function as an antecedent can be assumed to hold for the abstract noun phrases that are the postulated antecedents for first- and second-person noun phrases in these cases as well. For most of these additional examples, there is considerable variation from idiolect to idiolect, and it has been argued (e.g., in Fraser, 1971) that this variability weakens or destroys the force of the arguments for which these have been placed in evidence. This need not be the case, since the abstract-performative hypothesis is supposed to be a linguistic universal. Every idiolect that I have checked has **some** spurious reflexives that support the analysis. I cannot see why the fact that there is apparently no one spurious reflexive whose distribution is the same for all speakers of English detracts from the evidence that they yield when all facts are considered together. I will do little more here than list the various spurious reflexives that commonly require overt antecedents for third-person pronouns but none for first- or second-person pronouns. The reader may determine for himself which of these support an abstract higher clause for his own dialect. All but the first of these were described by Ross (1970).

In some idiolects, the second of two conjoined noun phrases is obligatorily reflexivized if it is coreferent with the subject of a higher clause, or if it is a first-person pronoun:

(13)   *ᵈBill and myself both have Hupmobiles.*

(14)   *ᵈEric said that Bill and himself both had Hupmobiles.*

For more speakers, sentences like the following are grammatical:

(15)   *ᵈZippora said that the machine gun was designed by Chaya and herself.*

(16)   *ᵈThis book was written by Linda and myself.*

After so-called "picture nouns" (e.g., *picture, portrait, book, story*), spurious reflexives occur in genitival prepositional phrases (see also Lees and Klima, 1963).

(17)   *Bill said that it was a picture of himself.*

(18)   *This is a picture of myself.*

Notice that if a clause intervenes between the antecedent and the spurious reflexive, the sentence is ungrammatical:

(19)   *Bill$_i$ said that Martha told Sally that it was a picture of himself$_i$.*

It is also the case that a sentence with the spurious reflexive in an extraposed subject clause is generally ungrammatical:

(20)   *Bill said that it was unlikely that it was a picture of himself.*

(21)   *It's unlikely that this is a picture of myself.

These facts support the conclusion that the abstract first-person noun phrase is in an immediately higher clause, and that the whole surface sentence functions as an object clause in semantic structure.

Clauses introduced by *as for NP+self* are grammatical for some if the reflexive is coreferent with subject of the next-higher clause, or if it is a first-person reflexive and introduces the highest surface clause:

(22)   ^d*Edgar decided that, as for himself, he'd take four sugars.*

(23)   ^d*As for myself, I prefer sloops to ketches.*

In one common dialect, however, a discourse referent is a sufficient conditioning factor, as in the following discourse:

(24)   *I just saw Renaldo.* ^d*As for himself, he looks pretty good.*

It is the set of idiolects in which (22) and (23) are grammatical but (24) is ungrammatical that lends support to the performative analysis. *As for NP+self* constitutes important evidence, since this construction alone among the spurious reflexives demands an antecedent in the **immediately** higher clause.

Besides the dialectally variable facts surrounding the distribution of spurious reflexives, there are also universal, or at least pan-English, data that lend credence to the higher-clause hypothesis. Consider, for example, the use of personal pronouns.

First of all, I wish to back up the traditional notion that the term "personal pronoun" does refer to a class of words that behave similarly. This may seem an entirely obvious point; but it has, in fact, been called into question on a few occasions—for example, in Sampson (1971). Personal pronouns of all three persons behave identically as far as the following processes are concerned: (a) They make the otherwise optional rules of dative movement and particle movement obligatory when they function as the object of an appropriate verb:

(25)   They sold $\left\{ \begin{array}{l} \left\{ \begin{array}{l} *him \\ *it \\ *me \end{array} \right\} you \\ \\ you\ to \left\{ \begin{array}{l} him \\ it \\ me \end{array} \right\} \end{array} \right\}$.

$$(26) \qquad They\ gave \left\{ \begin{array}{l} \left\{ \begin{array}{l} me \\ him \\ you \end{array} \right\} away \\ \\ *away \left\{ \begin{array}{l} me \\ him \\ you \end{array} \right\} \end{array} \right\}.$$

(b) Personal pronouns are required as the subject of a sentence with an introductory topic phrase:

$$(27) \qquad Bill,\ \left\{ \begin{array}{l} he \\ *Bill \\ *George \end{array} \right\} \text{'s a size 16.}$$

$$(28) \qquad Me,\ \left\{ \begin{array}{l} I'm\ a \\ *linguists\ are \\ *Jerry's\ a \end{array} \right\} Democrat.$$

$$(29) \qquad You,\ \left\{ \begin{array}{l} you\ don't \\ *Bill\ doesn't \end{array} \right\} \text{ have to worry about taxes.}$$

(c) Personal pronouns reduce in a special way when followed by the clitic 'll in rapid speech (see Zwicky, 1970).

(30)   I'll [al]
            you'll [jʊl]
            he'll [hIl]
            they'll [ðɛl]

(31)   Cy'll [sajəl] (*[sal])
            Hugh'll [hjuwəl] ,*[hjʊl])
            Bea'll [bijəl] (*[bIl])
            Ray'll [rejəl] (*[rɛl])

Thus, at some stage of derivation, the whole set of personal pronouns must share some structural characteristic so that processes like those just portrayed can be stated in their fullest generality.

There are two distributionally distinct kinds of contexts in which third-person personal pronouns occur. In one they alternate with full noun phrases with the same referent, and in the other, only the pronoun can be found.

$$(32) \qquad Bacon_i\ believed\ in\ heating\ by\ antiperistasis$$

$$and\ \left\{ \begin{array}{l} Bacon_i \\ he_i \end{array} \right\} was\ brilliant.$$

$$(33) \qquad Icarus_i\ thought\ that\ \left\{ \begin{array}{l} he_i \\ *Icarus_i \end{array} \right\} could\ fly.$$

The conditions under which a particular referential noun phrase must show up as a third-person pronoun are well known (see Langacker, 1969 or Ross, 1967). Stated briefly, a noun phrase **must** appear as a personal pronoun if it is preceded by a coreferential noun phrase in the same or in a higher, nonconjoined clause. If the situation in (34) obtains at the appropriate stage of derivation, the noun phrase NP_2 must appear as a personal pronoun if NP_1 and NP_2 are coreferent.

(34)

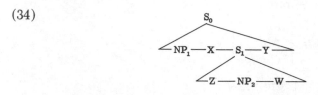

Now, first and second-person pronouns are, in general, the only noun phrases that can refer to the speaker and addressee of a sentence. They do not alternate with full noun phrases with the same referent, and they occur in the same syntactic environments as those in which obligatory third-person pronouns occur. All of the instances of obligatory personal pronouns can be treated uniformly under the higher-clause analysis. If S_0 in structure (34) is the abstract-higher-performative clause, then any noun phrase in the surface sentence will be in the position of NP_2. Then if a noun phrase in a surface sentence refers to either the speaker or the addressee, it will necessarily appear as a first- or second-person pronoun, for exactly the same reasons that obligatory third-person pronouns appear.

The treatment of the category of person is itself considerably simplified by the higher-clause analysis, as shown by Harada (1970). In an earlier transformational treatment, that of Postal (1966), the person of a noun phrase was a function of three independently variable syntacto-semantic features, "±I," "±II," "±III." As Harada argued, this treatment requires a number of ad hoc assumptions, including the following:

(35)   No noun phrase can be marked $[-I, -II, -III]$.
(36)   If the noun phrase is singular, only one feature may be specified positively.
(37)   No plural noun phrase can be marked $[-I, -II, -III]$.

Then, in order to specify the morphological realization of a noun phrase bearing an allowable combination of feature specifications, rules like the following would be required, and would have to apply disjunctively in the mentioned order:

(38)   NP ⟶ [first person] / [+I]
(39)   NP ⟶ [second person] / [+II]
(40)   NP ⟶ [third person]

However, the rather ad hoc restrictions (35), (36), and (37) can be dispensed with entirely if we trace person specification to the abstract higher clause. Assuming that the referential index of a plural noun phrase is the conjunction of the indices of the individual entities to which it refers, á la McCawley (1968), then rules (41), (42), and (43), which are analogous to (38), (39), and (40), respectively, account for all of the facts of personal referring expressions that have been mentioned. These rules must also apply disjunctively and in order.

(41)

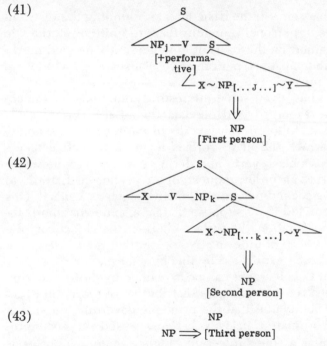

(42)

(43)   NP

                    NP ⟹ [Third person]

Rule (41) is to be interpreted as marking any noun phrase as a first-person noun phrase if its referential index includes a specification identical to that of the subject of the performative clause. Rule (42) applies if rule (41) has not, to mark a noun phrase as second person if its index contains a specification identical to the indirect object of the performative clause; and rule (43) marks all noun phrases to which neither (41) nor (42) has applied as third person. The state of affairs that had to be specified by assumption in (35), (36), and (37) results automatically from this treatment.

Harada's scheme also unifies a description of a language like Eskimo that has a fourth-person category morphologically parallel to
the first, second, and third persons. A fourth-person noun phrase
occurs in embedded clauses or their remnants if the noun phrase is
coreferent with the subject of the main clause of the sentence (see,
for example, Schultz-Lorentzen, 1969). The specification of the
fourth person in Eskimo would be similar to that of first and second
persons, except that it mentions the main clause and not the higher
performative clause. Without higher abstract clauses, the fourth
person alone would be marked on the basis of syntactic environment,
while the other personal specifications would have to be assumed to
be underlying.

We see, then, that some of the basic facts surrounding the distribution and reference of personal pronouns that are quite mysterious in
isolation are explained on the basis of independently needed mechanisms when higher abstract performative clauses are included in
underlying structures.

R. Lakoff (1968) has given some interesting arguments for the abstract-performative theory, based on data from Latin. Very briefly
stated, she argues as follows: Many verbs in Latin demand complement clauses in which the main verb is in the subjunctive mood.
Among these are, as a class, verbs of ordering. Now, one of the standard ways of effecting an order, request, or suggestion in Latin is to
use a free-standing second-person subjunctive, such as *Venias*! This
form could be predicted if we suppose that, at a somewhat more abstract level of representation, the surface clause is the object complement of an abstract verb of ordering. Note, too, that the sense of the
sentence would also be explicated by this hypothesis.

Another fact that Lakoff argues can be explained by the assumption
of abstract performative clauses is the distribution of the Latin negatives *ne* and *non*. She claims that the principle governing the use of
these items in subordinate clauses is that *non* is used if the subordinate clause functions as the **subject** of a higher sentence, but *ne* is
used in subordinate **object** clauses. Now, *ne* is also found in independent subjunctives with imperative force, and in negative imperatives. This, she argues, can be explained on the basis of the
hypothesis that these clauses were subordinate object clauses at an
earlier stage of derivation.

While this theory is attractive, it does suffer one serious deficiency.
The ordinary negative element in declarative sentences is *non*, not
ne. Yet the abstract-performative theory demands with equal force
that declarative sentences, as well as imperatives, arise ultimately

from object complements of higher abstract verbs. The performative theory, coupled with Lakoff's analysis of Latin, would therefore predict, falsely, that *ne* would be found in negative declaratives just as it is in negative imperatives.

One interesting way out of this dilemma would be to postulate that declaratives in Latin are, in fact, subject clauses. Appropriate abstract predicates would be of the class exemplified by the English adjectives *true* and *certain*. It would, then, be these abstract predicates which are the immediate object clauses of the abstract declarative verb, as in (44).

(44)

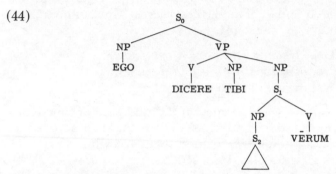

Remember, though, that Ross adduced evidence for English in support of the claim that declarative sentences function as the **objects** of higher abstract verbs. Is there, then, a profound difference between the logical structures of Latin and English? Not necessarily. The arguments for the object nature of declarative sentences are, as far as I can see, flawed. On the basis of the following sort of paradigm, Ross concluded that the antecedent for spurious reflexives after picture nouns (see p. 25) had to be in the next-higher clause.

(45) *Bill said that it was a picture of himself.*
(46) **Bill said that it was unlikely that it was a picture of himself.*
(47) *This is a picture of myself.*
(48) **It's unlikely that this is a picture of myself.*

But this paradigm is not complete. Certain clauses can intervene between the clause containing the antecedent and the clause containing the spurious reflexive. Interestingly enough, a clause containing the predicate *true* is of this type:

(49) *Bill said that it was true that it was a picture of himself.*

(50)   *It's true that this is a picture of myself.*

On the basis of this slim hint, I timorously suggest that it is possible that English, too, has an underlying predicate TRUE in the abstract logical form of declaratives. Note that such an operator in logical structures could help explain the aspects of natural languages that indicate the operation of a two-valued logic. No language I know of, for example, displays three responses to positive yes–no questions, one indicating belief that the questioned proposition is true, one indicating belief that the proposition is false, and one indicating the feeling that the proposition lacks a truth value. English, for example, employs *no* in either of the last two cases. Thus, either (52) or (53) is a well-formed answer to (51).[1]

(51)   *Does Newton still have a pet gecko?*
(52)   *No, he traded it for a gila monster.*
(53)   *No, in fact, he never did.*

This is exactly what we should expect if a truth operator functioned in English yes–no questions and in assertions, for such an operator turns three-valued logic into two-valued logic according to the following table (see, for example, Horn, 1972):

(54)

S	TRUE(S)
T	T
F	F
O	F

An argument similar in flavor to the subjunctive argument has been given for imperative sentences in English by McCawley (1968). As is well known, imperative sentences suffer deletion of a second-person subject. This is borne out by paradigms like the following, whose import has been thoroughly discussed in the literature.

(55)   *Shave* $\left\{ \begin{array}{l} *myself \\ yourself \\ himself \end{array} \right\}$.

(56)   *Shave* $\left\{ \begin{array}{l} me \\ *you \\ him \end{array} \right\}$.

---

[1] I am indebted to David Dowty for this observation.

(57)
$$Nod \begin{Bmatrix} *my \\ your \\ *his \end{Bmatrix} head.$$

What sort of mechanism is it, though, that guarantees that imperative sentences always have second-person subjects? In Katz and Postal's (1964) treatment, for example, there would have to be an entirely unique and ad hoc semantic well-formedness constraint that marks underlying structures as ill-formed if they contain the imperative morpheme associated with a highest clause whose subject is not a second-person noun phrase.

At the same time, there are independently required constraints on the subjects of subordinate clauses. These constraints always involve the nature of the verb in a higher clause. Thus, any propositional object of the verb *try* must have the same underlying subject as the verb *try* itself. There are no sentences like

(58)   *Byron tried (for) Shelley to swim the Bosphorus.

but only sentences like

(59)   Byron tried to swim the Bosphorus.

in which the underlying subject of the clause with the verb *swim* (deleted at some point) refers to Byron.

Similarly, there are verbs that take indirect objects as well as sentential direct objects, and impose constraints on the subjects of their complement clauses. For the most part, these demand that the subject of the object clause and the indirect object of the matrix clause be coreferent. Verbs of ordering (*order, request, tell* [in the sense of "order"], *ask* [in the sense of "request," "command," etc.]. are of this type. There are no well-formed sentences like

(60)   *I requested Sam for Marty to take out the garbage.
(61)   *I requested of Sam that Marty take out the garbage.

Some speakers find (61) almost grammatical, but only when it means "I requested of Sam that he make/let Marty take out the garbage." The constraint under discussion holds for this interpretation, too.

Under the abstract-performative hypothesis, an imperative sentence would be the propositional object of a verb of just this class. Since, by definition, the indirect object is a second-person noun phrase, the constraint operative for verbs of ordering—that their indirect object and the subject of their clausal direct object must be coreferent—**predicts** that only second-person subjects can occur in imperative sentences. There is no need whatsoever for special restrictions or assumptions.

ADVERBIAL EXPRESSIONS

We now also have an explanation for the fact, mentioned in the previous chapter, that sentence adverbs do not occur with imperative sentences. It has been supposed that adverbs in general are reduced versions of higher clauses (Geis, 1970; G. Lakoff, 1970c) — that is, that the following pairs of sentences are closely related:

(62a)   *The neutron was discovered in 1932.*
(62b)   *The discovery of the neutron took place in 1932.*
(63a)   *Fortunately, Chichester resigned.*
(63b)   *That Chichester resigned is fortunate.*

Thus, certain sentences with adverbs are thought to begin life as the subject clauses of predicates that express adverbial ideas. As far as sentence adverbs are concerned, this is always the case. But remember that the abstract performative verb of ordering demands, as do all verbs of its semantic class, that its indirect object and the subject of its complement clause be coreferent. An imperative with a sentence adverb would have to stem from a structure such as (64). But this structure ˙does not meet the condition on semantic well-formedness, since NP_i, which refers to an individual, cannot be coreferent with NP_k, which is a proposition.

(64)

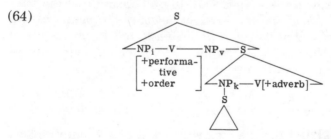

Semantically well-formed imperatives, then, cannot have sentence adverbs.

It is also tempting to trace the lack of an overt subject in imperative sentences to general principles, rather than postulate a special rule to account for this phenomenon. Notice that the majority of the verbs of ordering allow the deletion of the subject of their sentential object. This is the result of the transformational rule of Equi–NP deletion, described briefly in Chapter 1. The rather rudimentary statement of the rule given there provided only for the deletion of subjects of subordinate clauses under identity with the subject of the next-higher clause. It is clear, however, that a more general statement of the rule would allow deletion of the subject of an object clause under identity with either the subject or the indirect object of the matrix clause. The condition on whether it is the subject or indirect object of the higher clause that controls the deletion is this (see Postal, 1970b): If the subject of the subordinate clause is necessarily coreferent with the subject of the matrix clause, then the subject of the matrix clause controls the deletion. If the subject of the subordinate clause is necessarily coreferent with the indirect object of the matrix clause, then the indirect object of the matrix clause controls the deletion. For example, one sense of the verb *promise* requires that its subject and the subject of its complement clause be coreferent:[2]

(65)   *I promise for Bill to go.*
(66)   *I promise to go.*

In (66), and in (67) as well, the subject of the verb *go* is understood as coreferent with the subject of *promise*.

(67)   *Harry promised Jane to go.*

Now, verbs of ordering as a semantic class require coreference between their indirect objects and the subjects of their complement clauses. Moreover, verbs of ordering that have indirect objects all allow Equi–NP deletion into their complements. The imperative transformation might, then, turn out to be nothing more than the independently needed rule of Equi–NP deletion operating between the indirect object of the higher performative clause and the subject of its complement sentence, as suggested by McCawley (1968). This possibility could then explain the otherwise surprising fact that in numerous languages there is a subjectless syntactic pattern that functions as does the English imperative. This coincidence would then be traceable to the fact that most, and quite possibly all, languages include Equi–NP deletion in their inventory of grammatical processes.

More evidence for the higher-clause analysis comes from the fact that there are adverbs and adverbial expressions whose distribution can be predicted on the basis of this theory, but not otherwise (see

---

[2] There is a homophonous verb *promise*, meaning roughly "to swear that it is true," that does not require coreference between its subject and the subject of its complement clause.

Sadock, 1969a). Consider, for example, sentence (68).

(68)   *For the last time, I don't like liver.*

It is obvious, first of all, that the adverbial phrase *for the last time* is not understood as modifying the sentence in the same way that it does in one interpretation of (69).

(69)   *For the last time, Ussorssuaq beheld his native land.*

In fact, *for the last time* cannot modify the propositional content of sentence (68), as is shown by (70):

(70)   **I don't like liver for the last time.*

This particular adverbial seems to cooccur only with nonstative verbs, but the verb in sentence (68) is stative. Performative verbs are, as a class, nonstative and, therefore, are all capable of being modified by *for the last time:*

(71)   *I promise, for the last time, to give you a bicycle for Chanukah.*
(72)   *I tell you for the last time that I don't like liver.*

Sentence (72) is a fairly close paraphrase of sentence (68), and we can thus see that the distribution of the adverbial is explained by the abstract-performative hypothesis. In a theory in which a higher clause of the appropriate kind is lacking, one would be required to claim, erroneously, that there are two homophonous adverbial expressions *for the last time*, one that occurs only with stative propositions and one that occurs freely—except before exclamations—as an introductory expression. Worse still, one would have to provide an interpretive rule that projected the underlying form of sentences containing the introductory expression onto semantic forms precisely analogous to those that underlie sentences containing the ordinary adverb.

There is a large (in fact, open-ended) class of **expositive,** adverbials—a term borrowed from Austin's (1965) classification of performative verbs—whose function is to modify the abstract performative in a way that will be examined more thoroughly in Chapter 3. These include such words as *first, secondly, finally, frankly, personally,* and phrases like *in conclusion, once and for all,* and *to begin with.* By assuming that these expressions have the same properties sentence-initially as they do when used sentence-finally—that is, by making no special assumptions at all—it is possible to determine quite accurately the properties of higher abstract performative clauses. The prepositional phrase *in conclusion,* for example, occurs grammatically only with verbs of linguistic communication. Two examples should suffice.

(73)   *Professor Smirk described, in conclusion, the mating habits of rotifers.*
(74)   **Julia baked, in conclusion, a zucchini cobbler.*

From the existence of grammatical sentences such as (75), then, we may safely conclude that the verb in the higher abstract clause is—quite naturally—one of linguistic communication.

(75)   *In conclusion, the verb phrase is a problem for grammarians.*

We may safely surmise that one of the properties of the higher abstract clause is that it is a performative clause. This aspect of the higher clause is also corroborated by the behavior of certain expositive adverbs. To see this, consider how the following two sentences are understood:

(76)   *I claim, in short, that pigs have wings.*
(77)   *I claimed, in short, that pigs have wings.*

In example (76), *in short* describes the claim; but in (77), *in short* describes the **description** of the claim. Adverbs like this, then, are interpreted as modifying the performative clause, whether it is overt or not. In order to specify this in a general fashion, the grammar will have to distinguish performative clauses from nonperformative clauses in some way, and ensure that both overt and abstract performative clauses are distinguished in the **same** way from nonperformative clauses.

Not all properties of overt performatives are so neatly shared by abstract performatives, though. For example, the adverb *hereby* occurs only with performative clauses.

(78)   *I hereby announce my retirement.*
(79)   **Bill hereby announces his retirement three times a year.*

But *hereby* is found only with **overt** performatives. Thus, we find (80) but not (81), and we find (82) but not (83):

(80)   *I hereby predict that we will have seven lean years.*
(81)   **We will hereby have seven lean years.*
(82)   *I hereby request that you submit a written complaint.*
(83)   **Hereby, submit a written complaint.*

Therefore, the distribution of *hereby* gives no evidence for the performativeness of the higher abstract clause.

There are occurrences of *hereby* in sentences that do not match the explicit-performative formula. Two examples are (84) and (85):

(84)   *You are hereby fired.*
(85)   *The meeting is hereby adjourned.*

It is apparent in these cases, though, that the sentences are versions of explicit performatives.[3]

Another sort of adverbial phrase that gives evidence for higher abstract performative clauses is the reason adverbial, the subject of careful study by Davison (1972). Consider, for example, the differing interpretations of sentences (86) and (87):

(86)   *Feta is made from goat's milk, since you wanted to know.*

(87)   *Feta is made from goat's milk, since there are few llamas in Greece.*

The clause beginning with *since* in (86) obviously does not explain why feta is made the way it is, while that in (87) does. Rather, it explains why the speaker is saying what he is. There is also a surface grammatical difference between these two sentences. In (87), a pause is optional before *since;* but in (86), the pause is obligatory.

If the *since* clause in (86) is associated with the performative clause in underlying structure rather than with the propositional content of the sentence, its sense is naturally explained. This source for the reason adverbial also explains the obligatoriness of the pause in (86), as opposed to its optional presence in (87). To see that this is so, examine the following sentences:

(88)   *Mr. Adams told Billy that bees pollinate flowers, since they're embarrassed about sex.*

(89)   *Mr. Adams told Billy that bees pollinate flowers since they're embarrassed about sex.*

Example (88) is ambiguous as to which clause the reason adverbial

[3] Part of the explanation for the fact that *hereby* shows up only with explicit performatives may lie in an observation made by Davison (1972). She noticed that covert performatives never function as the anticedent for anaphoric processes. While the following is grammatical: *I promise you a tricycle for Christmas because your mother wants me to/even though I shouldn't do so/etc.*, similar sentences with abstract performative verbs are ungrammatical: *°You can have a tricycle for Christmas because your mother wants me to/even though I shouldn't do so/etc.* Thus, if the adverb *hereby* is analyzed as an anaphoric device, its behavior follows from more general principles.

modifies. It has either a reading in which Mr. Adams' embarrassment resulted in his watered-down relation of the facts of life, or one in which the bees' shyness was claimed to cause them to pollinate flowers. Sentence (89) has only the latter reading. Therefore, some mechanism must be provided to insert a pause between a dependent clause and a following reason adverbial that is associated with a higher clause. This independently required mechanism, whatever it might be, will then automatically prefix a pause to the *since* clause in (86) if this clause is associated with a higher abstract clause in underlying syntactic structure.

Questions conjoined with *or* and preceded by a pause can be appended to any sentence, with an effect reminiscent of that of reason adverbials. Nearly synonymous sentences result from adding an *if* clause of opposite polarity from the *or* clause:

(90)   *Who was the first German to visit Patagonia, or don't you know?*

(91)   *Who was the first German to visit Patagonia, if you know?*

(92)   *Pay the gas bill, or don't you have the time?*

(93)   *Pay the gas bill, if you have the time.*

(94)   *A ketch has two masts, or did you know that?*

(95)   *A ketch has two masts, if you didn't know that.*

Once again, the sense of these sentences can be explicated by associating the parenthetical clauses with an abstract performative clause. And it is not necessary to make the undesirable claim that the *or* and *if* that occur in sentences like (90)–(95) have no relationship to the *or* and *if* that operate on the surface propositional content of sentences. This would be an especially embarrassing claim in the present instance, since the relationship between *if* and *or not* in the preceding examples is tantalizingly reminiscent of the conditional law operative in English that accounts for the near synonymy of the following two sentences:[4]

(96)   *If Scrooge had a quarter he would have given it to Donald.*

(97)   *Scrooge didn't have a quarter or he would have given it to Donald.*

An interesting residual problem involves making explicit the relationship between the question form of the *or* clause versus the

---

[4] These facts were pointed out to me by Jean Ehrenkranz LeGrand.

nonquestion form of the *if* clause in examples (90)–(95).

It should be observed that different sorts of reason adverbials and parenthetical *if* and *or* clauses are appropriate for different sorts of illocutionary acts, whether these are explicitly represented in terms of an overt-performative formula or not. In the case of nonexplicit performatives, this fact helps strengthen the view that these parenthetical qualifiers are, indeed, associated with an abstract performative clause at a higher level of structure, rather than with the part of the content of the sentence that finds its way to surface structure. The parallelism among the following sentences arises naturally from the theory of higher clauses:

(98a) *I request that you close the door, since I'm busy.*

(98b) *Close the door, since I'm busy.*

(99a) ?? *I maintain that Columbus landed in Hoboken, since I'm busy.*

(99b) ?? *Columbus landed in Hoboken, since I'm busy.*

(100a) *Tell me what the specific gravity of osmium is, if you're so smart.*

(100b) *What's the specific gravity of osmium, if you're so smart?*

(101a) *I claim that Eskimo is an ergative language, or did you know that already?*

(101b) *Eskimo is an ergative language, or did you know that already?*

The reason and condition clauses just discussed are clearly related to the felicity conditions on illocutionary acts. Reason adverbials state that a felicity condition has been met, or in what way it has been met. For example, for an assertion to be felicitous, the speaker must have reason to believe that what he says is true. Thus, we can put forth in a reason adverbial appended to a statement the mode in which the knowledge was obtained:

(102) *Goats can fly,* $\begin{cases} because\ one\ once\ landed\ on\ our\ roof \\ since\ my\ mother\ told\ me\ so \end{cases}$.

Postsentential *or* and *if* clauses call into question felicity conditions that the speaker has reason to believe have not been met. Ordinarily, these must be **hearer-based** conditions (Gordon and Lakoff, 1971), for the speaker presumably knows whether he himself has fulfilled the prerequisites that are incumbent upon him for the felicitous performance of his own speech act. Thus, following assertions, we can have such clauses as *if you want to know* and *or did you* *know that?*, and following requests, such expressions as *if you don't mind, or don't you want to?*, and so forth.

Because of the relationship between these speech-act adverbials and the felicity conditions on illocutionary acts, their study can be enormously enlightening as to the speech-act value of various sentence forms. For example, the illocutionary force of exclamations, which comprise a special sentence type in English, is not immediately obvious. But the illocutionary value of exclamations is fairly clearly shown by the range of speech-act adverbials with which they cooccur. This range is tightly circumscribed, and includes principally adverbials that call into question whether the addressee holds the same point of view as that proclaimed in the exclamation. Specifically excluded are adverbials that are typical of assertions that reinforce the speaker's assumption that the addressee does not already know what he is being told. Thus, compare (103) and (104) with (105).

(103) *What a scorcher* (!), $\left\{ \begin{array}{l} \textit{or haven't you been outside yet?} \\ \textit{*in case you didn't know.} \end{array} \right\}$

(104) *Is she ever tall* (!), $\left\{ \begin{array}{l} \textit{or don't you think so} \\ \textit{*or did you know that already} \end{array} \right\}$?

(105) *It's about 75° out,* $\left\{ \begin{array}{l} \textit{?or haven't you been outside yet} \\ \textit{?or don't you think so} \\ \textit{or did you know that already} \end{array} \right\}$?

It is clear that these exclamations do not have the informative status of assertions.[5] While they commit the speaker to a particular view, they are not used, and cannot be used, to inform, enlighten, or instruct. In that they are noncontroversial by nature, exclamations of this kind serve a social function. They point up a commonality between speaker and addressee, which, however trivial, helps lay the groundwork for further conversation.

RESPECT LANGUAGE

The facts surrounding respect language in various languages provide a fertile source of evidence for higher performative clauses.

---

[5] The existence of a very different sort of exclamation, which more closely resembles an assertion, was noticed by James McCawley. These are used to convey surprising new information. Compare the behavior of the following sentence with respect to felicity-condition adverbials with that of examples (103) and (104):

> *Smith defect to Albania? — or do you have information*
> I don't?/ *or haven't you read the papers lately?

Numerous languages demand that a speaker make reference to his rank, age, or social status **relative to the addressee** when speaking. The facts surrounding respect language thus point to the existence of noun phrases in the semantic form of sentences that refer to the speaker and to the addressee. That respect language is at least partially a grammatical phenomenon can be appreciated by noticing that the inconsistent use of respect language results in ungrammaticalness. The following sentence, for example, is ungrammatical in German, since it uses the polite second-person form of address in one place and the familiar in another:

(106)   *Sagen Sie mir ob du fertig bist.[6]
                   ("Tell me if you are ready.")

Any grammar of German would have to provide some means of excluding sentences like (106) while including the two corresponding grammatical variants, *Sag mir ob du fertig bist* and *Sagen Sie mir ob Sie fertig sind*. Two brute-force methods of accomplishing this would be (a) to have only [−polite] noun phrases in deep structure and provide the grammar with a transformational rule that applies optionally to mark all second-person noun phrases in a single sentence [+polite], or (b) to include an arbitrary politeness morpheme in the semantic structure of sentences, on the basis of the presence or absence of which the polite or familiar second-person pronouns are subsequently chosen. Of these, only the second alternative is available in a semantically based grammar such as the one advocated in this book, for sentences with polite pronouns are not interchangeable in a given context with the corresponding sentences with familiar pronouns.

The relationship between the speaker and his addressee can show up directly in vocative expressions. When this is the case, there is little question which form of address is appropriate. Both of the following sentences are perceived as deviant by speakers of German:

(107)   ?? *Warum haben Sie mich verlassen, mein Gott?*
         ("Why have you [polite] forsaken me, my God?")
(108)   ?? *Wie hast du geschlaffen, Herr Kapitän?*
         ("How did you [familiar] sleep, my Captain?")

Under the assumptions of the performative analysis, noun phrases referring to the speaker and to the addressee are present in the underlying form of every sentence. These could bear status markers that would obviate the necessity for a special politeness morpheme,

---

[6] This fact was called to my attention by Arnold M. Zwicky.

since all of the relevant information regarding the relative status of speaker and addressee would thus already be present. This system is especially convenient for the treatment of languages like Korean, with very complex systems of honorification.

In Korean,[7] honorification involves the use of nominal endings, verbal infixes, and special lexical items. The choice of these items depends on what the speaker perceives to be the relationship between himself and the addressee, on the one hand, and some third person mentioned in the sentence and the addressee, on the other. Thus, for example, the verbal infix *-imni-* is used if the speaker wishes to indicate that the addressee is his social superior (elder, etc.); the verbal infix *-si-*, on the other hand, is used if the speaker wishes to indicate that the person to whom the subject of the verb refers is the speaker's social superior. Notice that, regardless of whether there is any overt reference to the speaker or to the addressee in the sentence, their status is important in determining the distribution of honorifying morphemes. For the status of a nonparticipant to exert a similar influence, however, he must be explicitly mentioned in the sentence.

But this is exactly the prediction that the theory of higher performative clauses makes, for these, by assumption, are associated with every sentence and contain noun phrases that refer to the speaker and to the addressee. Thus, every sentence contains noun phrases that could be marked as indicating the relationship between speaker and addressee. If the status designated by elements of surface morphology were interpreted on the basis of these morphemes, no explanation for the state of affairs we find in Korean would be forthcoming. An interpretive rule could just as easily be made to account for a hypothetical language in which deference could be shown toward the addressee's maternal grandmother regardless of whether she is mentioned in a sentence or not. Such an interpretive rule would also run afoul of the fact that if honorific morphemes are found embedded in clausal objects of verbs of linguistic communication, comments about status are made relative to the subject and object of the *verbum dicendi* (as shown by Lee and Maxwell, 1970). The interpretive rule would, therefore, have to involve two distinct parts, one for highest surface clauses and one for clausal objects of verbs of saying. Notice that the higher-clause hypothesis explains all cases uniformly, since highest clauses are assumed under it to function as the objects of abstract verbs of linguistic communication.

[7] I wish to thank Chin-Wu Kim for telling me about the relevance of Korean honorification, and Kiyong Lee for many useful comments on the subject.

It is, in fact, fairly common for languages to use attributes of the speaker and of the addressee to determine surface morphology, whether or not appropriate noun phrases are present in the surface form of the sentence. One especially interesting case was described by Sapir (1958). In Yana, a phonological rule applies to every word in a main clause, devoicing the final segment of the word. The rule applies just in case one or more of the participants in the discourse is a woman. In quotations, however—the objects of verbs of linguistic communication—the rule applies if either the subject or the indirect object of the higher clause refers to a woman.

MISCELLANEOUS SYNTACTIC AND SEMANTIC ARGUMENTS

The similarity between reports of explicit performatives and reports of sentences whose illocutionary force is covert can be explained by an appeal to the abstract-performative analysis. There are a number of verbs that can be used to report both the force of an utterance and, in their complements, the content of the utterance. Explicit performatives can generally be reported simply by appropriate adjustment of any deictic elements in the original utterance. Each of the following (b) sentences can be used to describe the corresponding (a) sentences in answer to a question like *What did he say?*

(109a) *I pronounce you man and wife.*
(109b) *Rev. Bernstein pronounced us man and wife.*
(110a) *I warn you that there are several bridges out.*
(110b) *Officer O'Brien warned us that there were several bridges out.*

Notice, now, that covert illocutionary acts can be reported in similar ways, such as

(111a)   *The dog is barking.*
(111b)   *My wife told me that the dog was barking.*
(112a)   *Did you sleep well?*
(112b)   *What's-her-name asked me if I had slept well.*

For the most part, verbs describing perlocutionary acts apparently cannot be used in this way. None of the following, for example, is grammatical.

(113)   *Bill lied that he would be here.*

(114) *Bill surprised us that he had been promoted.
(115) Bill misled us that there was a lion in the bushes.
(116) *Officer O'Brien scared us that he warned us that
         there was a lion in the bushes.
(117) *Rev. Bernstein doomed us that he pronounced us man
       and wife.

There are verbs, such as *convince*, that do take *that* complements, but clearly report a perlocutionary effect of a declarative-form utterance. It is clear, however, that they do not report the content of an utterance. For this reason, a sentence like (118b) cannot be used to report an occurrence of (118a) in answer to the question, *What did the secretary say?*

(118a)   Omaha is in Ohio.
(118b)   He convinced us that Omaha is in Ohio.

Another thing that distinguishes the (b) sentences in examples (109)–(112) from (118b) is their potential use as **proxy speech acts.** Present-tense sentences analogous to (109b), (110b), (111b), and (112b) can be used by an interlocutor (or interpreter) to convey both the content and the force of the corresponding (a) sentences (or their equivalents in a foreign language) to the intended addressee. But an interpreter could hardly translate the German equivalent of (118a)—say, by turning to the person the speaker of (118a) intended as his addressee and saying,

(119)   He convinces you that Omaha is in Ohio.

   Another point of confusion involves verbs that report not only the illocutionary force and content of an utterance, but also the manner in which the utterance was made (see Zwicky, 1971).

(120) The senator blurted out that he owned an antiaircraft
       gun.

Once again, such sentences can be distinguished from straight-forward reports of speech acts in that they cannot be used as proxy speech acts, nor in answer to a question like *What did he say?*

   Given the abstract-performative-clause analysis, a uniform account of the appropriateness of the report of an utterance can be given. We need only say that the report is appropriate if it asserts that an act has taken place that corresponds to the performative clause in the semantic representation of the original utterance. In the case of overt performatives, this clause will have been represented in both surface and semantic structure, but otherwise the crucial structure will have been present only at an abstract level of representation. In the absence of abstract performative clauses, one would be forced to give a two-pronged account of the appropriateness of the report of utterances. In the case of overt performatives, the theory would include the single uniform statement of the abstract-syntactic theory. But for illocutionary forces that do not surface as explicit performatives, an entirely separate, interpretive statement would have to be made.

Another sort of fact that helps motivate higher abstract performative clauses concerns the often observed fact that sentences like (121) are ambiguous as to who is responsible for the description in the relative clause (see McCawley, 1970b).

(121)   *Bill said he dislikes the man who has a Mogen David-shaped wart on his nose.*

In one understanding, the description is attributed to the referent of the subject of the higher clause, in this case Bill; but in the other understanding, the description is attributed to the speaker of the sentence. This latter sense, which has been termed the **referential sense** by Donellan (1971), is the one we find when (121) reports Bill's having said, for example, *I dislike Alfred*. Now, notice that sentence (122) is three ways ambiguous as to who is responsible for the description embodied in the relative clause:

(122)   *Bill said that Sam told him that he dislikes the man who has a Mogen David-shaped wart on his nose.*

Sam, Bill, or the speaker of (122) can be responsible for the attribution in this case.

Disregarding complicating factors that are irrelevant to the present argument, we see that whatever account is given of responsibility for a predication, it will have to allow responsibility to be attributed to the referent of the subject of a higher sentence that contains a verb of linguistic communication. Because of this, assignment of responsibility to the speaker of a sentence will proceed automatically under the terms of the abstract-performative hypothesis, since the speaker of the sentence is the referent of the subject of a higher clause that contains the right kind of verb. An account of these facts without higher abstract performative clauses, however, would fail to capture this generalization. Indeed, such a treatment has recently been given by Hasegawa (1972), who explicitly rejects the performative analysis. Hasegawa writes two quite distinct rules of "assertor" assignment, one that deals with noun phrases present in the surface form of the sentence, and one for the speaker of the sentence.

A topic related to the specification of responsibility for a description is that of the scope of the pragmatic operator. Consider, in this regard, examples (123) and (124):

(123) *Ronald asked whether Bruce had managed to inflate the bagpipe.*

(124) *Ronald asked whether Bruce was surprised to have inflated the bagpipe.*

In (123), we understand Ronald's question to have been about both Bruce's inflating the bagpipe and his managing to do that. In (124), on the other hand, we know that Ronald assumed that Bruce had, in fact, performed the Scots miracle and was asking only whether that fact surprised Bruce. This difference in the scope of the pragmatic operator *ask* has to do with the nature of the verbs *manage* and *surprise* in the dependent clauses. *Manage* is what Karttunen (1971) has called an **implicative verb**; it is transparent with respect to a higher predicate. Given any structure of the form (125),

(125)

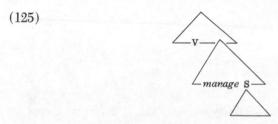

part of the meaning of the sentence in which (125) occurs is always (126):

(126)

Now, notice how the following sentences are interpreted:

(127)   *Ronald managed to play a piobareachd.*
(128)   *Did Ronald manage to play a piobareachd?*

Uttering (127) includes the **assertion** that Ronald played a piobareachd, and uttering (128) involves asking whether he did. It is clear that *manage* is also transparent to whatever illocutionary act is performed upon it. The precisely parallel behavior of *manage* and other verbs of its ilk with respect to overt higher predicates and with respect to illocutionary force argues strongly that illocutionary force ought to be treated as a higher predicate.

Compare the behavior of *manage* with that of the so-called **factive verb** (Kiparsky and Kiparsky, 1970) *surprise*. Example (124) does not entail the assertion that Ronald asked whether Bruce inflated the bagpipe. In fact, we know from (124) that Ronald assumed that Bruce had done it.[8] In fact, this is true regardless of what verb is substituted for *ask* in (124). It is the case for factive verbs, then, that part of the meaning of any sentence that contains a substructure like (129) can be represented as (130).

(129)

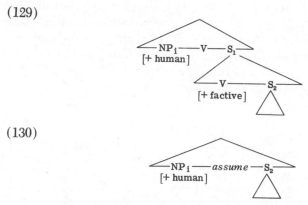

(130)

Once again, there is a strict analogy between the behavior of certain verbs in complement clauses and their behavior in highest surface clauses. Consider the interpretation of (131) and (132):

(131)   *Bruce was surprised to have inflated the bagpipe.*
(132)   *Was Bruce surprised to have inflated the bagpipe?*

Both (131) and (132) have as part of their meaning an assumption on the part of the speaker of the sentence that Bruce inflated the bagpipe. The higher-abstract-clause proposal allows one to treat factive verbs in subordinate clauses and factive verbs in main clauses in a uniform way. A main clause, under this hypothesis, has the function of S_1 in a structure like (129), where the [+human] noun phrase refers to the speaker of the sentence. Therefore, since (130) is always

---

[8] The discussion of factive verbs presented here is necessarily highly simplified. Thus, in another reading, (124) involves the **speaker's** assumption of the truth of the complement of *surprised* as well. The existence of additional readings, though, should not affect the worth of my argument. For a more detailed discussion of quasi-logical predicates, see Karttunen (1973).

a part of the meaning of sentences containing structures like (129), nothing special has to be said in order to account for the meaning of main clauses containing factive verbs.

There are numerous expressions and constructions in any natural language that require for their understanding that the context—that is, the speech-act situation—be brought in. Thus, *here* in sentence (133) means, approximately, "to the place at which this utterance is being made."

(133)   *Marat often bathed here.*

Such **deictic elements,** or **shifters,** as Jakobson (1971) has called them, give evidence for abstract syntactic material just in case there are demonstrably related processes that demand overt syntactic material for their occurrence and interpretation. One such case has already been discussed in this chapter. First- and second-person pronouns are deictic elements; since they are obligatory pronouns (see page 27 ff)—a category that, in all other cases, requires a grammatical context—they support an analysis in which the appropriate grammatical context is present at an abstract level of representation. An extensive treatment of deixis is well beyond the scope of this book. Consequently, I will give only one argument based on it in favor of the higher-abstract-clause hypothesis as a model.

In dependent clauses, tense refers to the time of the event, relative to the time of the matrix clause. From example (134), for instance, we understand that Gorm's riding of an eohippus predated his realization of that fact.

(134)   *Gorm realized that he had ridden an eohippus.*

Partially because of the existence of facts like this, McCawley (1971) suggested treating tense as an underlying two-place predicate. Past tense would then have a meaning something like "prior to." In McCawley's scheme, the past-tense morpheme is realized as *have*, unless it is in a context where subject-verb agreement applies to it. Furthermore, all but the first of a series of occurrences of this *have* are deleted. Now the point is that, for dependent clauses, both the arguments of tense morphemes are present, but in main clauses, this does not seem to be the case. Note, though, that the sense of corresponding tense morphemes is quite the same in main and dependent clauses. Sentence (135) tells us, among other things, that the time at which the act of writing occurred preceded the time of the speech act.[9]

[9] This generalization was made by Reichenbach (1966:296n).

(135)   *Sam wrote me a letter.*

According to the view that nonperformative main clauses are the deep objects of higher performative clauses at an earlier stage of derivation, all[10] instances of tense and its reflexes can be handled uniformly. In all cases, the arguments of the underlying tense predicates would be the time of the occurrence or existence of the event or state in the subordinate clause, and the time of the occurrence or existence of the event or state in the superordinate clause.

SUMMARY

None of the arguments given in this chapter is, by itself, entirely convincing. It is possible to pick each apart, find fault with the data, find new data that do not quite fit, and so on. Yet the fact remains that the volume and range of the evidence make the higher-performative hypothesis one of the better-supported abstract-syntactic theories. There are, on the whole, fewer problems per argument in this case than there are in the case of, say, the passive transformation.

This one semantically useful thesis allows the capture of numerous unrelated syntactic and semantic generalizations, as we have seen. Since it is this sort of generalization upon which modern formal grammar is based, it is always surprising that the idea of abstract performatives has met, and continues to meet, stiff resistance from generative grammarians in every camp. I hope to have shown, though, that the wide-ranging utility of the higher-performative-clause analysis far outweighs its sole supposed drawback, extreme abstractness.

I wish to point out, in conclusion, that the merits of the idea do not reside solely in its ability to capture semantic and syntactic generalizations. Important additional benefits derive from the fact that it is a formal theory. As such, it binds us to certain empirically testable hypotheses, and the testing of these hypotheses, in turn, rewards us with insights into linguistic pragmatics that would be difficult or impossible to achieve otherwise. As with all theories, this one is bound to turn out to be wrong. But in order to show where it goes astray, the theory forces us to ask significant questions, in a rational order, about the use of sentences in communicative situations, and thus to widen and deepen our understanding of how it is, exactly, that we manage to communicate.

[10] This statement is clearly much too strong. There are many examples that are not easily amenable to the treatment described here. Some of the more intransigent cases are discussed in R. Lakoff (1970).

3

Embedded Performatives

In the simple version of the abstract-performative theory, it is assumed that a performative clause is in absolute highest position in semantic representations. This postulate is based on the observation that clauses of the performative type ordinarily lose their performativity when embedded. None of the following sentences, for example, could constitute a promise. With the performative adverb *hereby*, they are therefore ungrammatical.

(1) *I think that I (*hereby) promise you a tricycle.*
(2) *I admit that I (*hereby) promise you a tricycle.*
(3) *It will shock you that/if I (*hereby) promise you a tricycle.*
(4) *The tricycle which I (*hereby) promise you is red.*

On the basis of data like these, Ross (1970) concluded that performative-like clauses that are embedded in surface structure never function performatively. It was quickly observed, however, that this blanket generalization, like most in grammar, does not hold (see Ross, 1969c; Sadock, 1969b; Fraser, 1971). There are numerous sorts of sentences in which an embedded performative clause does, indeed, do what it says. Some examples follow.

(5)   *I regret that I must inform you that your goldfish has died.*

(6)   *It pleases me that I am able to announce my candidacy.*

(7)   *I wish to announce that I hereby tender my resignation.*

Example (5) can be an act of informing, (6) an act of announcing, and (7), among other things, an act of resigning.

It is also necessary to consider as an embedded performative any performative whose surface form indicates that there was a higher clause at some earlier stage of derivation. It has, for example, been convincingly argued by Ross (1969a) that modals and other auxiliaries arise from higher clauses, in which they function as main verbs. Apparently, then, performative sentences like the following point to earlier structures in which the performative clause is one of the arguments of a modal predicate.

(8)   *I must caution you not to tease the dragon.*

(9)   *I can assure you that no effort will be made on your behalf.*

(10)   *I should point out that the two sentences above are performatives.*

Assuming that (8) contains the transitive, or root, modal—that is, the one paraphrasable as *is required*—rather than the intransitive, or epistemic modal, which is roughly synonymous with *is necessarily true,* it would have roughly the structure given in (11) earlier in its derivation. The question of whether there ought to be a performative clause dominating S_0 will be disregarded for the time being.

(11)

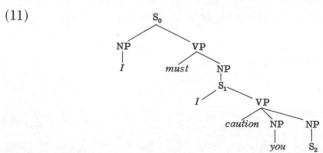

More obviously derived from embedded structures are infinitive phrases, among which many sorts of examples of seeming performatives can be found. In the following examples, the embedded performative verb is underlined.

(12) *I regret to <u>inform</u> you of the death of your goldfish.*
(13) *I am required to <u>ask</u> the purpose of your visit.*
(14) *My firm has allowed me to <u>offer</u> you a year's supply of
      TV dinners in exchange for your silence.*

Well-known and widely accepted arguments exist that would demand that (14), for example, be derived from a structure essentially like (15) at a slightly more abstract level, neglecting again the problem of a higher abstract performative clause above S_0 (see Rosenbaum, 1967).

(15)

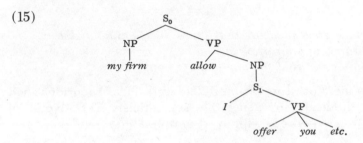

Here too, then, it is apparently an embedded clause, S_1, that accounts for the illocutionary force of the sentence.

According to the performative hypothesis itself, the aspects of surface form that differentiate interrogative and imperative sentences from declarative sentences are traceable to a higher abstract clause. The lack of a subject in imperative sentences, for example, was attributed in Chapter 2 to the presence of a coreferent noun phrase functioning as the indirect object of a higher abstract clause. Yet there are numerous examples of apparently performative sentences with the surface form of interrogative and imperative sentences:

(16) *Let me assure you that this is skim milk and not cream.*
(17) *May I point out that there are no languages with only
      340 words?*
(18) *Be warned that straining methanol through bread will
      not make it potable.*

The surface clause in (18) that indicates explicitly that the sentence is a warning must, according to the performative analysis, be dominated at an earlier stage of derivation by a higher abstract clause containing a verb of the semantic class of *request* and an indirect object that refers to the addressee, which triggers the deletion of the coreferent subject of the complement clause.

It appears that, for the sake of consistency, it must also be assumed that at some stage an abstract assertive clause dominates the structure, giving rise to a sentence like (14). The clause in (14) that indicates that it is an offer is, thus, at least two clauses from the top of the tree on some more distant level. Similarly, since (17) contains a modal auxiliary and is interrogative in form, the clause responsible for its pointing out is at least two sentences distant from the root of the tree at a somewhat more abstract level. Sentences can be found in which the apparently performative clause is embedded to a depth of three, as in (19) or (20), or more. There seems, in principle, to be no limit to how deeply such clauses may be embedded, or at least there is no principle of which I am aware that would define such a limit.

(19)   *It is with great pleasure that I am able to announce the acceptance of your application.*
(20)   *Let me be the first to congratulate you.*

Finally, as mentioned in Chapter 2, adverbs have been identified with higher predicates by generative semanticists. Yet adverbs of many types regularly occur with overt performatives:

(21)   *I cordially invite you to attend.*
(22)   *I humbly request that you consider my suggestion.*
(23)   *I gratefully acknowledge your gift.*

A declarative sentence parallel to (21), such as (24), would ordinarily be analyzed as having a semantic structure somewhat along the lines of (25) (see G. Lakoff, 1970c).

(24)   *Stalin cordially invited Berla in for a chat.*

(25)

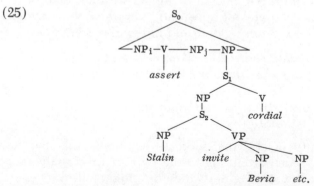

Since, in (21), the clause with *invite* as its main verb is the performative clause, there is no need, nor apparent motivation, for postulating the existence of an **abstract** performative clause. Without making any further assumptions, this leaves (21) with a semantic structure like

(26), as far as the underlying hierarchical arrangement of clauses is concerned.

(26)

```
                          S₀
                       /      \
                    NP          V
                    |           |
                    S₂        cordial
                  /    \
                NP      VP
                |      /  | \
                I  invite NP  NP
                          |    |
                         you   S₂
```

In all of these cases, we see that fairly well-established syntactic theory clashes head-on with one of the basic tenets of the performative analysis: The performative clause responsible for the illocutionary force of a sentence is assumed to be the highest semantic clause, yet in these cases it is clearly not the highest clause at a more remote level of structure.

There are two major lines of attack one could adopt in order to resolve this dilemma. The first is to assume, following Sampson (1971), that what looks like the illocutionary force of the embedded clauses in each of the preceding and in any similar examples is actually only a perlocutionary effect. The second way of avoiding the paradox would be to assume that surface-embedded performatives derive somehow or another from underlying highest clauses. Both ideas have some validity in isolated cases. The notion that certain surface-embedded clauses are unembedded at the level of semantic representation has, in fact, fairly widespread utility. But there remain, as I will show, some intractable examples of embedded performatives that neither scheme can explain away without resort to fairly bizarre and unwarranted mechanisms. In these cases, then, one is forced to modify the simple abstract-performative analysis in such a way as to accommodate embedded performatives in the right places.

Let us examine the first strategem, that of writing off the apparent force of embedded performatives as perlocutions. In the case of, say, sentence (19), the claim would be that the only illocutionary force of the sentence is that of an assertion. The speaker of (19) merely informs his addressee that some ability of his gives him pleasure, and it is only as a by-product of this assertion that the utterance amounts to an acceptance of an application. Similarly, following the perlocution ploy, sentence (20) would be assigned the illocutionary force of a question so that the sentence could be used to congratulate only as a perlocutionary aftermath of its asking something.

In the two cases just given, this strategem has at least a modicum of plausibility. There are other examples, however, where it is extremely counterintuitive to deny that an embedded clause corresponds to a performative structure. Of course, the problem of distinguishing illocutionary force from perlocutionary intent or effect is an extremely subtle one. The whole of Chapter 5, in fact, will be devoted to this question. Here, I simply wish to cast doubt on some of the specific conclusions to which we are forced by an attempt to identify illocutionary force always with the highest apparent clause or with an abstract clause immediately above it.

Let us take an example. Suppose that Art Frambes receives a letter from his insurance company that contains the following sentence:

(27)   *We regret to inform you that your policy is canceled.*

Suppose that a week later Frambes' Vespa is crushed by a carved cornice falling from a Louis Sullivan building that is being demolished. He applies for reimbursement under the falling-object clause of his insurance policy, and is told that the policy has been canceled and that he has been duly notified of that action. In the subsequent suit, Mr. Schuster, Frambes' attorney, argues that he was never notified of the cancelation of his policy and that he is therefore entitled to collect for his loss. The counselor freely admits that Frambes received a letter from Mutual of Hoboken, but it simply stated that the company had certain negative feelings and did not inform the victim that his policy had been canceled, as required by law.

Who wins? Pretty obviously, the insurance company does. Sentence (27), despite Mr. Schuster's protestations, can be used to perform an act of informing its addressee of the cancelation of his policy. Notice, also, how we might report the content of the letter Frambes received. Example (28), for example, seems honest and accurate.

(28)   *Mutual of Hoboken informed Mr. Frambes of the cancelation of his policy.*

But (29) is inaccurate, or at least incomplete, and (30) is ungrammatical:

(29)   *Mutual of Hoboken expressed their regret about informing Mr. Frambes of the cancelation of his policy.*
(30)   **Mutual of Hoboken regretted to inform Mr. Frambes of the cancelation of his policy.*

Recall that it was suggested in Chapter 2 that the link between a speech act and a report of that act is the performative clause, real or abstract, in the semantic form of the sentence that was used to accomplish the original act. Therefore, since (27) can be honestly reported by (28), it would seem that the underlying clause whose main verb is *inform* is, after all, a performative clause.

Notice, moreover, that one way of canceling an insurance policy is to inform the policyholder of the cancelation. Thus, (31) is also an accurate report of what the company did in writing to Frambes.

(31)   *Mutual of Hoboken canceled Frambes' policy.*

The act described in (31) also has the character of an illocutionary act. The insurance company, having written (27), could hardly deny that it intended to cancel the policy. Moreover, the performative adverb *hereby* can occur grammatically in (27) in the clause with the verb *cancel:*

(32)   *We regret to inform you that your policy is hereby canceled.*

It therefore seems likely that (27) has at least double illocutionary force: It is an act of informing and an act of policy cancelation. Double illocutionary force in a stack of clauses is certainly inconsistent with the highest-performative-clause doctrine. Indeed, part of the motivation for this doctrine was that, in the most obvious cases, a single, nonconjoined sentence carries one and only one illocutionary force.

Although the acts indicated by the embedded clause in examples (5)–(27) resemble illocutionary acts in that, having uttered the sentences, one cannot deny that they have been performed, and in the way in which they can be reported, it is still possible to remain a proponent of the thesis that these are, nevertheless, perlocutionary forces. A good deal of squirming would be required, though. First of all, one would have to draw a distinction between ordinary, hit-or-miss perlocutionary effects and perlocutionary effects that are unavoidably entailed by illocutionary acts of certain types. In the preceding examples, the perlocutionary effects in question would be of this automatic variety. Because such perlocutions necessarily accompany utterances of a certain kind, and because speakers of the language are aware of this constant conjunction, they would always be communicated acts. A formal theory of how utterances are reported could then state that all communicated acts—that is, both semantically marked illocutionary acts and perlocutionary effects whose accomplishment is automatic upon the utterance of a sentence—can be reported, without editorializing, by asserting the occurrence of the act described by the appropriate verb.

As unwieldy as this system is, and as much as it enfeebles the distinction between illocutionary and perlocutionary acts, it still does not adequately characterize sentences like (5)–(27). This is because there exist automatically entailed perlocutionary effects that are, intuitively at least, quite distinct from the automatic effects of embedded clauses like those under discussion. No distinction between them could be drawn under the patched-up theory just presented. Consider, for example, the following sentence:

(33)   *Alex hasn't found out yet that your chicken was run over.*

If the addressee was not aware of the fact that his chicken had been run over before (33) was spoken to him, he certainly would be afterwards. This is because *find out that* is a factive predicate, one that presupposes the truth of its complement clause. A speaker can sincerely utter (33) only if he believes the proposition expressed by the *that* clause to be true. If the addressee is a speaker of English, he knows this as well. Thus, one automatic consequence of uttering sentence (33) is to lead the addressee to believe that the speaker believes that the clausal object of the sentence expresses a true proposition. This clearly perlocutionary effect is quite automatic, and very similar to an illocutionary act of assertion. Yet in this case, there is no possibility of misregarding it as an illocutionary act.

It might be objected, at this point, that the obvious difference between (33) and, say, (27) is that the latter contains a clause that explicitly indicates what the automatic perlocution is, while (33) does not. Notice, first of all, how much the distinction between the two kinds of automatically accomplished perlocutionary effects is coming to resemble the distinction between illocutionary and perlocutionary acts. Moreover, consider the following sentence:

(34)   *Arthur told me not to mention that he's in town.*

This is unavoidably a mention of the fact that Arthur is in town. But (34) is by no means an ordinary or straightforward way of mentioning that fact. Certainly, (34) must be distinguished from (27) in some way, and that way would seem to be to regard the embedded clause in (27) as a performative—as the source of the illocutionary force of the sentence—but to maintain that the dependent clause in (34) merely produces an automatic perlocutionary effect.

A further fact that would be very difficult to explain without calling some embedded clauses performatives is the following: Certain matrix structures **require** that their complements have all of the salient properties of explicit performatives. An archexample of this sort is the verb *regret* with an infinitival complement. Note that, if the complement contains a verb in any other form than the infinitival reflex of the simple present, or if the verb is not a potentially performative verb of the semantic class of *inform*, the sentence is ungrammatical:

(35)   *I regret to $\begin{Bmatrix} be\ announcing \\ have\ announced \\ be\ going\ to\ announce \end{Bmatrix}$ my resignation.

(36)   *I regret to $\begin{Bmatrix} \begin{Bmatrix} blurt\ out \\ reveal \end{Bmatrix} that\ you're\ fired \\ brush\ my\ teeth \end{Bmatrix}$.

It is also the case that the subject of the verb *regret* and the subject of the complement clause must be coreferent:

(37)   *I regret for the department to announce that the course is closed.

And there are restrictions on the range of allowable subjects of *regret* in this construction. Basically, the subject must be a referring expression pure and simple:

(38)   Bill regrets to announce that he won't be here today.
(39)   *Anyone regrets to announce that the meeting is adjourned.
(40)   *People with red hair regret to announce that the negotiations have broken off.

Finally, notice that (38), while grammatical, has an unusual interpretation: It can be used only as a proxy speech act—as a way of accomplishing Bill's announcement for him. .

All these facts can be accounted for directly by claiming that the complement clause in these examples is a performative.

Other predicates that demand performative-like complements are *be pleased* and *be sorry*, with infinitival complements. These predicates ordinarily take factive *that* complements; but when they do, their complements are generally not performative:

(41)   I am pleased that I offer you a case of Scotch as a token of my gratitude.

In fact, it is difficult to find a context in which this sentence is

appropriate. At any rate, the nonperformativity of the complement of
(41) follows from its factivity. Performatives, it should be recalled,
are not subject to judgments of truth or falsity, and factive complements are presupposed to be true. Therefore, we should expect to
find no factive complements that are performative. For the same
reason, a large number of **nonfactive** predicates (Kiparsky and Kiparsky, 1970), such as *be likely, be certain, believe, doubt*, and so on,
cannot take performative complements because they discuss the
truth value of their complements. Notice, also, that the complement
clause in (41) can be made performative by adding the modal auxiliary *can*. This is partially understandable because of the fact that
modals are nonfactive predicates, and therefore the propositions they
take as arguments are not presupposed to be either true or false. In
addition, when the complement of *can* is tenseless, the modal does
not comment on the truth value of its complement. It would be difficult, indeed, to explain the effect of the modal on the interpretation
of these embedded clauses without assuming that some are, in fact,
performative, which status makes them incompatible with truth-
value contexts.

In the case of performatives containing adverbs, an attempt to
claim that performative clauses are always highest by calling the
principal force of these sentences perlocutionary seems most ill-ad-
vised. The most extreme examples are those with the typical performative adverb, *hereby*. Presumably, the source of this element is a
higher instrumental predicate. G. Lakoff (1968) has argued that a sentence like *Max cut the salami with a knife* has a semantic structure
rather like the surface structure of the sentence *Max used a knife to
cut the salami*, at least in respect to the hierarchical arrangement of
predicates in the tree. By extension of Lakoff's conclusion to the example at hand, we would be drawn to propose that the semantic form
of an explicit performative such as (42), which contains the vocable
hereby, parallels the surface form of sentence (43).

(42)   *I hereby resign.*
(43)   *I use this sentence to resign.*

There are several fairly plausible possibilities concerning the remote
structure of sentences with instrumental adverbs, and all, as far as I
can see, would entail that the performative clause in a sentence like
(42) is embedded at this deep level. Structure (44) represents one
guess as to the semantic structure of (42). Here, the subject clause, S_1,
is the source of the surface main clause, and the verb phrase, VP_1, is
the deep source of the adverb *hereby*. One advantage of this proposal

is that it begins to explain the fact that *hereby* is transparently an anaphoric device, for in (44), the source of the adverb contains a noun phrase, NP_3, in an obligatorily pronominalizable position.

(44)

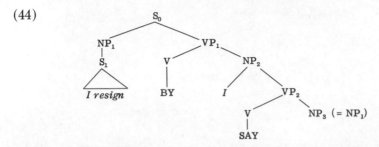

Now, sentence (42) is an archetypical performative. Thus, an attempt to reconcile the embeddedness of the performative clause at an abstract level with the thesis that performative clauses are always highest by claiming that the effect of this sentence is perlocutionary amounts to a *reductio ad absurdum*. For a number of independent reasons, then, it must be recognized that there are embedded performative clauses.

Let us now examine the second strategem for resolving the conflict between ordinary syntactic theory and one postulate of the abstract-performative hypothesis. This involves the claim that, while embedded reflexes of performative clauses undeniably exist at many levels of derivation (including surface structure), they do not exist on the level of semantic structure. Thus, the original thesis that illocutionary force can be attributed to a highest performative clause in **semantic structure** would still be tenable. In all cases where a performative clause is found embedded, then, rules of the grammar will have to be shown to have operated in such a way as to bring about the desired topological state of affairs.

In many instances, this maneuver has a ring of truth to it, despite the fact that it has its difficulties. Consider, for example, the case of sentence (12), which I repeat here for convenience as (45).

(45)   *I regret to inform you of the death of your goldfish.*

As was argued earlier, the illocutionary act performed in uttering this sentence is one of informing. We may safely surmise that, at a somewhat earlier stage of derivation, (45) has a syntactic structure approximately like (46). The derivation from structure (46) to surface structure is quite straightforward, and presents no new problems. However, structure (46) itself would differ considerably from its semantic

(46)

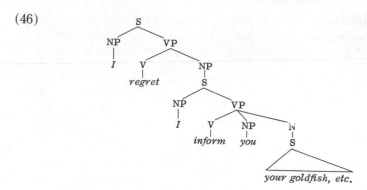

your goldfish, etc.

structure if the performative clause is to be highest on the level of sentence meaning. The first problem, then, is to figure out an appropriate semantic structure for (45) that meets the requirement that the clause whose main verb is *inform* is highest, and is such that the intermediate stage represented by (46) can be derived from it in a principled way.

One idea that suggests itself is simply to eliminate the offending higher clause from the semantic representation. But postulating the resulting semantic source for (45) is tantamount to claiming that the sentence is identical in meaning to the ordinary performative, (47).

(47)   *I inform you that your goldfish has died.*

Moreover, eliminating all clauses from logical structure that have the unfortunate quality of dominating performatives in derived structure would lead to the prediction that (48) is also synonymous with (47) and, consequently, that (45) and (48) are synonymous.

(48)   *I am happy to tell you that your goldfish has died.*

Both results are, obviously, absurd. The usual senses of the predicates *regret* and *be happy* are certainly a part of the meaning of (45) and (48), respectively. These predicates, or, more accurately, their semantic ancestors, must therefore find their way into the semantic form of these sentences.

With an eye to determining how *regret* is involved in the semantic structure of (45), notice the following peculiar fact about the meaning of that sentence: While it appears to express the speaker's regret at performing an illocutionary act of informing, it actually commits him to the claim that he regrets the death of a goldfish. This observation accords with the fact that the following sentence can be appropriately used only by a sadist:

(49)   *I am happy to tell you that you will be in excruciating pain for two weeks.*

and why (50) is appropriate if spoken to a rival.

(50)   *I regret to tell you that you've won.*

A substructure resembling (51) should, therefore, probably be part of the semantic representation of a sentence like (45).

(51)

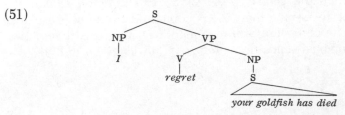

your goldfish has died

Now, structure (51) is not a performative structure. The verb *regret* is a stative verb, and no performative verbs are. Thus, one can always report a performative in terms of a pseudo-cleft sentence, a structure typical of nonstative verbs. A felicitous utterance of (52) can be reported as (53).

(52)   *I pronounce the meeting closed.*
(53)   *What he did was pronounce the meeting closed.*

Therefore, the fact that sentence (54) is ungrammatical suffices to show that *regret* is a stative, nonperformative verb.

(54)   **What he did was regret (to inform me) that my goldfish had died.*

Other arguments against the performativity of *regret* are easy to come by. This verb does not, for example, occur with *hereby*, nor does it occur in the *by* adjunct of expositive performatives.

(55)   **I hereby regret the passing of your pet.*
(56)   **I begin by regretting the passing of your pet.*

If, then, (51) cannot be a performative in itself, it must be embedded into a performative clause, since it has some speech-act value. Sentence (45) is, in part, an expression of regret, and it would therefore seem appropriate to embed the subtree (51) in an abstract performative clause containing a verb of the semantic class of *express.* One of the semantic restrictions on this class of verbs (besides, of course, that it must be a possible performative verb) is that it must take factive complements. Notice that the same restriction operates in determining the possible verb in the surface **complement** of *regret*. Thus, both of the following sentences are odd:

(57)   ?? *I claim that I regret the death of your goldfish.*
(58)   ?? *I regret to claim that your goldfish has died.*

One way of explaining the similarity between the infinitival surface complement of *regret* and the range of higher abstract performative clauses for which the clause $_s[I \ regret \ S]_s$ can function as complement would be to assume that (51) is conjoined to the object clause of the verb of the class of *inform* in semantic structure. A schematization of this proposed semantic structure of (45) is given in (59).

(59)

A subsidiary advantage of this proposed structure is that it does not contain an embedded performative, which is a desirable result in view of the difficulties encountered in claiming that performative clauses are not highest clauses.

Now, structure (59) must eventually be transformed into structure (46). Substructure S_2 in (59) must make a long jump and wind up dominating S_0. The details of the required "Jesse Owens" transformation are fairly obscure. I will simply state its overall effect in the rather ad hoc fashion of structure (60).

The necessity for such an enormously powerful and unique transformation as (60) is a serious drawback to the proposal under consideration. It is possible, though, that some of the burden of the crudely stated rule just given will be carried by already-existent rules. For example, the fact that the derived structure resulting from the application of the rule contains only one occurrence of S_1, whereas the input structure contains two, might be a function of well-known rules that serve to reduce repeated portions of conjoined structures. At present, this is mere speculation, however, and the fairly wild transformation that this treatment obliges us to assume weighs heavily against the advantages of the scheme.

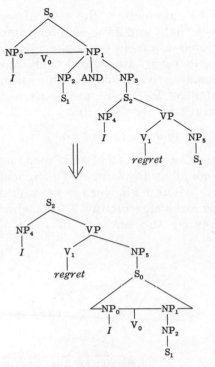

At any rate, it is the case that the statement of rule (60) does not require any mention of the class of the verb in S_0. The only structures that are semantically well-formed and meet the structural requirements of the input to rule (60) are exactly those containing a verb of the semantic class of *inform*. The proposition REGRET (I, S) can be directly embedded only into performative clauses of the required type, as example (57) and the following examples show:

(61)   *I inform you that I regret that your goldfish has died.*
(62)   *?? Do I regret that your goldfish has died?*
(63)   *?? I assert that I regret that your goldfish has died.*
(64)   *?? I suggest that I regret that your goldfish has died.*

Since S_0 is undominated, it must be a performative clause under the strong version of the higher-performative-clause analysis. S_1 is directly embedded into S_0 as a conjoined object, and therefore the verb in S_0 can only be a member of the class of factive-complement performative verbs of informing. Since S_0 will eventually wind up as the complement of *regret* through the agency of the Jesse Owens transformation, the restrictions on these complements are automatically accounted for. Provided that the conspicuous difficulties with this proposal can be surmounted, the case of sentences like (45), then, would provide only apparent counterexamples to the thesis that illocutionary force resides in the highest semantic clause.

Other examples, however, are considerably more intractable. In particular, performative sentences with speech-act adverbials present thorny problems for the highest-performative doctrine. Let us examine, in this regard, sentence (65).

(65)   *First of all, I promise to give you a new unicycle.*

Following the same strategem as that employed for the *regret to* class of sentences, we could try to claim that in semantic structure, the performative clause whose main verb is *promise* dominates the adverbial clause. The resultant structure is (66), which, inspection will show, is an appropriate structure for (67), and not for (66) at all.

(66)

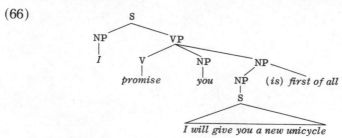

(67)   *I promise you that I will first of all give you a new unicycle.*

Practically the only remaining option is to factor out the adverbial and conjoin it to the *promise* clause along the lines of (68). Even in this structure, though, the performative clause is not absolutely highest:

(68)

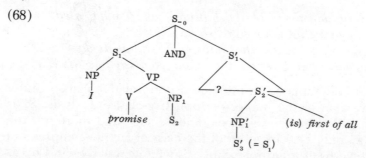

This move does hold out the hope for explanations of some distributional facts, as did the treatment of the *regret to* class of sentences. But another unmotivated and athletic rule would be needed to boot the entire first conjunct, S_1, into S'_1 in place of S'_3. Again, such a rule requires a good deal of justification, which is not at present available.

It is tempting to try to reduce the power of the required rule by allowing already-motivated grammatical rules to do part of the work. For example, we might want to attribute to the rule of conjunction reduction the fact that the semantic form has two occurrences of the same proposition (S_0 and S'_2) in separate conjuncts, while the surface sentence includes this proposition only once. Now, Davison (1972) has demonstrated that conjunction reduction fails to operate just in case the antecedent is an abstract performative:

(69)   *I accept your offer and I thank you for the opportunity of being able to.*

(70)   **You've won and I thank you for the opportunity of being able to.* [i.e., say that you've won]

Therefore, while (65) is partly explainable in terms of conjunction reduction, sentences with speech-act adverbials but no overt performative clause would seem not to be.

Given a semantic form such as (68), we are forced to fret about the nature of the verb in S'_0. That is, we must ask what the separate illocutionary force of the second conjunct is. It does not seem correct to say, for example, that part of the meaning of sentence (65) is the same, or nearly the same, as that of the assertion in (71).

(71)   *My promising to give you a new unicycle is the first thing of all I do.*

Rather than *assert*, a factive predicate more like *indicate* or *point out* seems in order here. If the person to whom a sentence like (65) is addressed disagrees with the proposition FIRST (S) (or whatever the appropriate proposition is), his reactions will be about the same as if he disagrees with a presupposition rather than a claim or assertion. Note, though, that a presupposition failure involving the speech-act adverbial does not nullify the whole speech act. Thus, if the third consecutive locution a speaker produces is (65), he is still bound by his promise. This fact could be explained by assuming an underlying structure, such as (68), that contains two separate illocutionary forces.

In the debit column for the coordinate-structure source for speech-act adverbials is the following interesting paradox:[1] Since (68) represents two consecutive speech acts, we would expect the succeeding ordinal adverbial to be *third(ly)* and not *second(ly)!* This is not a very

---

[1] I am indebted to James D. McCawley for calling this strange fact to my attention.

serious criticism, though, since, under most circumstances, we are allowed to assign a single ordinal to a series of illocutionary acts.[2] I find the following sequence of sentences perfectly acceptable:

(72)   *First of all, I'd like to welcome you and wish you a pleasant stay in Peoria. Secondly, I'd like to thank you for coming.*

A more telling argument against the coordinate semantic structure of sentences with speech-act adverbials is this: It is generally possible to switch addressees between conjoined speech acts. This is what the higher-performative-clause hypothesis would predict, since the addressee is the referent of the indirect object of the performative clause under this theory. Thus, sentence (73) is perfectly grammatical, while (74) is not.

(73)   *I want you, Bill, to cover the alley and you, Frank, to stay here.*

(74)   **I want you, Bill, to dance with you, Mary.*

It is also possible to change addressees between conjuncts, even when the underlying conjunctive form has been altered transformationally. For example, nonrestrictive relative clauses, as mentioned earlier, are generally believed to stem from underlying sentence-level conjuncts. The following sentence is grammatical, as the combination of these observations would predict:

(75)   *Tilly, I'll give you a ride in my Bugatti, which you know I have, Enzio.*

But addressees cannot be switched between a speech-act adverb and the body of a sentence:

(76)   **Finally, Jack, you're fired, Bill.*

(77)   **First of all, Henry, I bet you $5 that Dick wears makeup, Morty.*

It is possible that there are kinds of conjunctions of speech acts where only one addressee is allowed. If it turns out to be true, as Morgan (1969) and D. Cohen (1972) have suggested, that presuppositions are to be represented as conjuncts separate from the rest of the sentence, then that is another case where addressees may not be changed between conjuncts.

---

[2] An exception to this principle was noticed by Jean Ehrenkranz LeGrand. When the Good Fairy grants us one wish, it cannot be for a house in the country, a sports car, a Nobel Prize, and the ability to carry a tune. These are four wishes. But a wish for a million dollars is one wish and not a million, since the sum is seen as a whole.

Remember, also, that a general treatment of tense requires reference to the performative clause. What is needed to get this scheme to work, however, is an adverbial that specifies the time of the speech act. This adverbial, an obligatory part of every well-formed semantic structure in English, would seem, again, to be a clause in which the performative clause functions as the subject (i.e., a higher clause). Here again, we might provide a separate conjunct as a source for the adverbial. But once more, the maneuver is ad hoc, and still leaves the performative clause one clause down from the top. Finally, it would seem to be the case that some lexical performative verbs include higher modifiers as part of their meaning. *Beg*, for example, might be claimed to mean something like "ask for humbly." In Chapter 7, I will argue that the verb *warn* must be represented semantically and deep-syntactically, rather like "to propose a course of action for the addressee on the ground that not following that course of action would result in a consequence that the speaker presumes the addressee would find undesirable." In these examples, an adverbial apparently dominates the performative predicate, too. The hypothesis that the semantic performative can be identified easily in semantic representation by virtue of the fact that it is highest must—alas—be abandoned.

If abstract performative clauses may be embedded in semantic structure, how may they be recognized? What accounts for the fact that the same conglomeration of semantic primes can in one sentence perform and in another merely predicate? To what can we attribute the fact that—subject to the provisos outlined in Chapter 1—there is but one illocutionary force to any simple sentence? In my article "Superhypersentences" (Sadock, 1969b), I suggested that not only could performatives be embedded, they were **always** embedded in semantic structure. I suggested that it was the nature of the verb in the matrix clause that determined whether or not a potentially performative complement was indeed performative.

There is, in fact, some syntactic evidence for such a higher clause. Indeed, some of this evidence is quite the same as that which helped argue for the existence of higher abstract performative clauses in the first place. In several cases, the same arguments can be given using explicitly performative sentences in place of the nonexplicit performatives in the original argument. If the original argument pointed to a higher abstract clause with such-and-such a property above the nonexplicit performative sentence, then the modified argument must point to an abstract clause with the same property above explicit performatives as well.

Recall, for example, that in Chapter 2, I traced the obligatorily pronominal character of noun phrases that refer to the speaker and to the addressee to coreferent noun phrases in an obligatorily pronominalizing position (that is, higher and to the left) in underlying structure. But noun phrases that refer to the speaker and to the addressee in explicit performative clauses are obligatorily pronominal, too. Thus, we must assume that there exist grammatical antecedents above and to the left of performative clauses as well. Several spurious first- and second-person reflexives show up in explicit performatives also. In some dialects (see page 24), the following paradigm exists:

(78)   *ᵈBill and myself welcome you.*
(79)   *ᵈI dedicate the next song to Mary and yourself.*
(80)   **Himself and I/myself welcome you.*
(81)   **I dedicate the next song to Mary and himself.*

The frame *by NP and NP* also allows spurious first-person reflexives in performative clauses in some dialects;

(82)   *ᵈYou are cordially invited by myself and the Department of Phrenology to a gala seance.*

The higher structure that dominates performative clauses and is responsible for their performing is liable to turn out to be rather complex, but one salient aspect of it seems clear: It contains the abstract agentive predicate, DO.[3] All performative verbs are agentive anyway, and the independent arguments for tracing agentiveness to a predicate DO apply straightforwardly to them. It is possible, for example, to reduce an explicit performative to *do so*, as in the following example:

(83)   *I've been asked to invite you to the Bar Mitzvah and I hereby do so.*

The use of an explicit performative can be reported by means of a pseudo-cleft sentence, such as

(84)   *What the jury did was find him guilty of begging the question.*

If, as I argued earlier, reports of illocutionary acts involve repeating the performative structure of the original utterance, then here we have evidence that the semantic form of the original utterance contained a predicate DO above the act-defining verb.

---

[3] This conclusion was announced independently in Ross (1969c).

Now, let us recall what sort of predicates external to the performative itself had to be postulated above the performative. These were all what could be loosely called adverbials, relations predicated of propositions. None of these are agentive, and so it appears that there is still an easy way to identify the part of the semantic representation of a sentence that accounts for its speech-act value, the performative clause: It is the highest clause that is the object of the agentive predicate DO.

4

Indirect Speech Acts

Consider once again a sentence such as (27) in Chapter 3, which I repeat here as (1).

(1) *We regret to inform you that your policy has been canceled.*

We found that, despite the surface form of this sentence, there is good reason to consider the clause whose main verb is *inform* to be the highest agentive clause in deep syntacto-semantic structure. From a more superficial point of view, however, (1) appears to be merely a description of the speaker's mental state. Based on this discrepancy between surface form and use, such sentences have been termed **indirect illocutions** (see Heringer, 1972).

The same rubric has been used to cover several other sorts of cases as well. It includes sentences like

(2) *I will never divulge the secret that the gold is buried in the outhouse.*

in which the illocutionary act of avowal (or whatever it is) necessarily entails a perlocutionary act of divulging. Note that there is no performative verb *divulge:*

(3)   *I hereby divulge the secret that Dick is balding.

In this case, there is no possibility of being led to the erroneous conclusion that (3) is an **illocutionary** act of divulging, for which we should assume an underlying **performative** clause containing the verb *divulge*.

But, of course, the effect of many illocutionary acts can be accomplished perlocutionarily, too. The principal effect of a request is to bring the addressee to the awareness that some action is desired of him, but there are numerous ways in which this can be accomplished besides by uttering an imperative sentence or an explicitly performative request. Sentence (4), for example, has, as a consequence of its successful performance, the same principal effect as an explicit request.

(4)   I want you to bury the turtle.

Are we to say that (4) is an illocutionary act of requesting, or, more accurately, that (4) is ambiguous between an assertive and a request sense? Put differently, should we assign two different semantic structures to (4), one in which the performative clause contains an abstract verb of asserting and one in which it contains a verb of requesting? This is not the only conceivable way of explaining the various uses of a sentence. We could claim that (4) has only one meaning, one semantic representation, in which the encoded illocutionary act is, say, an assertion. Then, the fact that (4) can have the effect of a request would be considered an entailed perlocution, derivable in some way from the meaning of the sentence.

An even less direct way of accomplishing the same thing as can be straightforwardly accomplished by saying

(5)   Bury the turtle.

or

(6)   I request that you bury the turtle.

would be to say something on the order of

(7)   The turtle is beginning to smell.

It is not immediately obvious in which of these cases, if any, we are dealing with sentences that can have the meaning of a request, and in which cases the use of the sentence as a request is a matter of entailments based on the meaning of the sentence.

Speech-act entailments were suggested by L. J. Cohen (1971), and studied in detail by Grice (1968) and within generative grammar by

Gordon and Lakoff (1971). Gordon and Lakoff sought to develop a set of **conversational postulates** that can be used in a speech-act calculus to derive entailed forces from meaning.

One sort of conversational postulate that they discuss is based on what they call **sincerity conditions**. These specify what is entailed by the sincere use of the various illocutionary forces. For example, for a speaker sincerely to request some action of an addressee entails, according to these authors, that the speaker wants the action performed, that the speaker assumes that the addressee is willing and able to perform the action, and that the addressee would not perform the action unless requested to. These are formulated as follows by Gordon and Lakoff—where Q is of the form FUTURE (DO [b, R]):

(8a) SINCERE (a, REQUEST [a, b, Q]) $\longrightarrow$ WANT (a, Q)

(8b) SINCERE (a, REQUEST [a, b, Q]) $\longrightarrow$ ASSUME (a, CAN [b, Q])

(8c) SINCERE (a, REQUEST [a, b, Q]) $\longrightarrow$ ASSUME (a, WILLING [b, Q])

(8d) SINCERE (a, REQUEST [*a, b,* Q]) $\longrightarrow$ ASSUME (a,–Q)

The authors divide these conditions into two types: those for which the subject of the entailed proposition (other than the one dealing with the speaker's assumptions) is the speaker—**speaker-based sincerity conditions**—and those for which the subject of the proposition is the addressee—**hearer-based sincerity conditions**. Only (8a) is speaker-based, while (8b), (8c), and (8d) are hearer-based.[1] Noticing that all of the following can be used to convey a request to take out the garbage:

(9a)   *I want you to take out the garbage.*

(9b)   *Can you take out the garbage?*

(9c)   *Would you be willing to take out the garbage?*

(9d)   *Will you take out the garbage?*

Gordon and Lakoff (1971:65) suggest the following principle:

(10)   One can convey a request by (i) asserting a speaker-based sincerity condition or (ii) questioning a hearer-based sincerity condition.[2]

Given the sincerity conditions of (8), then, Gordon and Lakoff provide the following conversational postulates for English:

[1] Gordon and Lakoff admit to fudging in regard to (8d).

[2] There are several additional fudges here, some of which the authors own up to. First of all, the first-order predictions of principle (10) would be that the following sentences can be used to get across requests:

(11a)   SAY (a, b, WANT [a, Q])* $\longrightarrow$ REQUEST (a, b, Q)
(11b)   ASK (a, b, CAN [b, Q])* $\longrightarrow$ REQUEST (a, b, Q)
(11c)   ASK (a, b, WILLING [b, Q])* $\longrightarrow$ REQUEST (a, b, Q)
(11d)   ASK (a, b, Q)* $\longrightarrow$ REQUEST (a, b, Q)

The asterisks in these formulas indicate that either the entailed sense or the underlying syntactic sense is intended, but not both.

To get this system to work, Gordon and Lakoff must also allow entailed senses to influence surface form. This is because certain aspects of surface form are correlated directly with the potential use of sentences, regardless of their sentence type. Thus, while (12) can be used either as a request for information or as a sort of weak negative suggestion, (13) has only the latter use:

(12)   *Why do you paint your house purple?*
(13)   *Why paint your house purple?*

To account for this and numerous similar facts (about which I will have much more to say), Gordon and Lakoff include in the grammar a set of **transderivational constraints,** rules whose application is partially conditioned by entailed meanings. They suggest (1971:73) (14) as one possible statement of the rule that disambiguates (12):

(14)   WHY YOU TENSE X ⇒ WHY X ONLY IF C∥⊢ unless you have some
        good reason for doing X, you should not do X.

        In [(14)], "C∥⊢" indicates that the application of the rules [sic] is rela-
        tive only to those contexts and conversational postulates such that
        they together with the logical structure of the sentence entail what is
        on the right side of "C∥⊢."

Gordon and Lakoff provide no means of telling when a particular force is entailed and when that force is part of the meaning of a sentence. They apparently operate under the assumption that it is the grossest aspects of surface form that give an indication of the illocutionary force of an utterance. In all cases that they discuss, inverted surface word order is taken as an indication of a higher abstract performative clause of asking, and the lack of a surface second-person

---

(a)   *I assume that you can take out the garbage.*
(b)   *I assume that you are willing to take out the garbage.*
(c)   *I assume that you won't take out the garbage.*

Now, the first two of these are functional requests, but are much less straightforwardly so than the corresponding sentences, (9b) and (9c). On the other hand, sentence (c) cannot function as a request at all. Gordon and Lakoff observe that they are not able to explain these facts. They also note that, to account for (9d), they must assume that the question corresponding to a negative proposition is positive. Finally, I must point out that the subjunctive modal *would* in (9c) is not explained by their assumptions.

subject as an indication of an underlying performative clause of requesting. In every instance, they treat a sentence with a highest non-performative clause of normal word order as being underlain by a structure containing a performative clause of asserting. I will call the hypothesis under which Gordon and Lakoff were apparently operating "the surface meaning (SM) hypothesis." In its extreme form, the SM hypothesis demands that there be a one-to-one and onto relation between encoded illocutionary force and gross surface form.

The extreme view at the other pole has not, to my knowledge, been advocated in the linguistic literature. Heringer (1972), however, does assume that, in a large number of cases, it is the use of an utterance that corresponds to its encoded illocutionary force. I will label the apparently advocate-free view that use always corresponds to meaning the UM hypothesis. Under the UM hypothesis, each of sentences (4)–(7) would be assigned a logical structure in which there is a performative clause of requesting. Sincerity conditions would also figure prominently in the UM treatment of indirect speech acts. Instead of serving to derive force from meaning, as they do under the SM hypothesis, sincerity conditions would be employed in the derivation of surface form from meaning. Thus, according to the UM view of indirect illocutions, the semantically encoded sense of a sentence such as

(15)   *Can you close the window?*

would be similar to that of the sentence

(16)   *I request that you close the window.*

when (15) is used with the force of (16). The semantic form of (15) and its surface form would be mediated by the sincerity condition on requests, which states that the speaker assumes that his addressee is capable of carrying out the requested action.

The third position for the treatment of indirect speech acts is the one that will be advocated in this book. It takes neither extreme stance, but in some individual cases agrees with the SM position, and in some with the UM position. The burden that falls to the proponent of this third position, which I will somewhat unfairly dub "the meaning-meaning (MM) hypothesis," is to provide a method for determining in which cases illocutionary force and gross surface form agree, and in which cases they do not. I will provide the outlines of such a method in the next chapter. Here, I wish to argue that only the MM hypothesis is tenable.

The common difficulty with both the SM and the UM theories is that they treat in the same way all utterances whose use and gross surface form do not correspond. In neither theory is there any particularly important difference between sentences (17) and (18):

(17)   *Can you close the door?*
(18)   *Are you able to close the door?*

Since both can be used with the effect of a request to close a door, the UM proposal would require that they receive the same underlying representation (i.e., that of a request). The SM theory would derive the request sense of both sentences as a speech-act entailment from logical question structures, and both theories would make use of the same sincerity condition (or conversational postulate) in accomplishing the respective mappings.

But there is a strongly felt intuitive difference between sentences (17) and (18). The former is a fairly forthright instrument for making the request, while the latter is sneaky. Sentence (18) is truly indirect, and using such a sentence with the intent of getting someone to do something borders on dishonesty. The MM theory, alone among the three, holds out a hope of accounting for this difference. The MM theory, in principle, allows sentence (17) to receive the semantic representation of a request, and (18) the semantic representation of a question. The use of (18) as a request would then be derivative of its meaning, as in the SM theory, while the use of (17) as a request would be a function of its having the meaning of a request, as in the UM theory. This accords well with our intuitions into the matter, but, more important, it accords well with syntactic data that will be produced in the next chapter. Each of the two theories that I wish to reject also suffers from its own idiosyncratic afflictions. I will examine the UM theory first.

As L. J. Cohen (1971) has observed, nearly any speech-act type can be conveyed by the use of another. For example, we can warn someone of the presence of a bear by uttering any of the following:

(19)   *There's a bear!*
(20)   *Isn't that a bear?*
(21)   *Look out for the bear.*
(22)   *I warn you that there's a bear in our midst.*
(23)   *I didn't know there were bears in these woods.*
(24)   *What a big bear!*
(25)   *I believe that's a bear.*

And so on, literally *ad infinitum*. Now, recall that when these are used with the intent and effect of an overt performative of warning, the UM theory requires that they all receive a similar semantic representation. Quasi-syntactic rules will then operate upon this meaning form to perform the rather drastic changes that are needed to produce the sentences just given, and all others that can be used to warn of the presence of a bear. These rules are distinct from rules of semantic well-formedness. They are of a formally distinct type, since they have semantic trees as input and (semantic?) trees as output. Rules of semantic well-formedness, on the other hand, have semantic representations as input and the answer *yes* or *no* as output.

It can immediately be seen that the UM hypothesis entails a duplication of **all** of the work of the semantic well-formedness constraints. For example, we could expand (25) into (26) by adding an adverb and preserve the warning force, but (27) is ungrammatical:

(26)   *I firmly believe that's a bear.*
(27)   **I quickly believe that's a bear.*

This pattern is, of course, already specified by rules of semantic well-formedness for assertions. But remember that (26) and (27) are not assertions under the UM hypothesis. The independently required rules of semantic well-formedness are irrelevant for distinguishing between (26) and (27), since under the UM hypothesis, the structures that underlie (26) and (27) contain neither the adverbs nor the verb *believe*. We are faced, then, with the unhappy result that all semantic constraints are repeated in the quasi-syntactic component required by the UM hypothesis in order to transform representations that correspond to force into representations that will ultimately yield appropriate surface forms. The more pleasant alternative is to abandon the strict UM approach.

Because of its mirror-image relationship to the UM proposal, the SM proposal results in the duplication of the work of the **syntactic** component, rather than that of the semantic component. Let us take an example.

Questions can be used with the force of assertions of opposite polarity (**erotesis**). Thus, (28) can be used with approximately the same effect as (29) and (30), with approximately the same force as (31) (for how approximately, see Chapter 6).

(28)   *Does anyone study Aristotle anymore?*
(29)   *No one studies Aristotle anymore.*
(30)   *Haven't I been good to you?*
(31)   *I have been good to you.*

Positive **queclaratives** like this (see Sadock, 1971) can sometimes be ambiguous with regard to the height of the negative in the associated assertion. Sentence (32), for example, can signify something like either (33) or (34):

(32)   *Does Jack want to be arrested?*
(33)   *Jack wants not to be arrested.*
(34)   *It's not the case that Jack wants to be arrested.*

Notice, now, that the following queclarative has an interpretation parallel to (33), but not one parallel to (34). Sentence (35) can signify something approximately equivalent to (36), but not (37).[3]

(35)   *Does Jack hope to be elected?*
(36)   *It's not the case that Jack hopes to be elected.*
(37)   *Jack hopes not to be elected.*

These facts are exactly parallel to the fact that (38) has the sense of either (39) or (40), whereas (41) has only the sense of (42), and not that of (43):

(38)   *Jack doesn't want to be arrested.*
(39)   *Jack wants not to be arrested.*
(40)   *It's not the case that Jack wants to be arrested.*
(41)   *Jack doesn't hope to be arrested.*
(42)   *It's not the case that Jack hopes to be arrested.*
(43)   *Jack hopes not to be arrested.*

The two senses of (38) have traditionally been handled in transformational grammar by supplying a cyclically ordered transformational rule, variously called "negative raising" or "negative transportation" (see, for example, Fillmore, 1963; R. Lakoff, 1969a; or Burt, 1971). This rule optionally moves a negative element up one clause under certain circumstances. One of the main conditioning factors governing the operation of the rule is the nature of the higher verb. In general, verbs expressing mental desire allow a negative predicate from a lower clause to be raised. The verb *want* is a regular member of this class, while *hope* is exceptional in not allowing a semantically lower predicate to be raised.

The distribution of senses of the queclaratives (32) and (35) could

---

[3] Of course, (35) uttered as something akin to an assertion is **consistent** with the class of contexts in which (37) is true since (36) is. The point here, though, is that (35) does not allow an interpretation such that the utterer could be accused of being wrong unless Jack hopes not be be elected. These observations hold, *mutatis mutandis*, for (41), (42), and (43) as well.

be automatically accounted for by the rule of negative raising, provided that the negative is included in the semantic form of these sentences. What would be required in addition is a rule of queclarative formation, part of whose effect is to transform a derived structure in which a clause containing a negative is immediately dominated by a performative of assertion into a question lacking that negative. This rule, which is required anyway for tag questions, will be discussed with greater precision in Chapter 6. The surface sentence (32) would arise in two ways under this scheme. In one case, both negative raising and queclarative formation apply during the derivation, but in the other, the negative element is associated with the highest clause under the performative anyway, and so only queclarative formation need apply. In the case of (35), however, negative raising is, as we have seen, inapplicable. There is, therefore, only one source for (35)—the one in which the negative is semantically higher than the verb *hope*. This mode of explanation is, of course, available only under the MM or UM theory, for it requires that the semantic form encode pragmatic (and propositional) information that differs from that apparently indicated by the surface form: The surface form appears to be that of a question, but the underlying abstract performative is more like an assertion. I have already argued that the UM hypothesis is untenable, and this means that the suggested explanation for the behavior of queclaratives can be accommodated only under the terms of the MM theory.

Consider, by contrast, what the SM theory is forced to say about queclaratives. According to this view, the semantic form of (32) and (35) would closely resemble their surface form, at least as far as the structural elements we are interested in are concerned. These sentences would, in particular, contain no negative predicate, and have a verb of asking in the highest clause at the level of semantic representation. The possible uses of sentences that resemble (33) and (34) for (32), and (36) for (35) would have to be derived by the application of rules of pragmatic interpretation operating on semantic structures. The required interpretive device would include a part that mirrors the syntactic rule of queclarative formation and renders it unnecessary. This postulate would interpret a question as an assertion with a negative in the highest clause of the complement of the abstract interrogative verb, and is thus exactly the reverse of the syntactic rule that it supplants.

But in addition, a further interpretive rule is required to lower just the negatives introduced by the rule under discussion into lower structures. This rule would have to be cyclic or iterative, for

(44)   *Does Jack believe that Bill wants to be arrested?*

is three ways ambiguous as a queclarative, with senses corresponding approximately to (45), (46), and (47).

(45)   *It is not the case that Jack believes that Bill wants to be arrested.*
(46)   *Jack believes that it is not the case that Bill wants to be arrested.*
(47)   *Jack believes that Bill wants not to be arrested.*

And this negative-lowering rule would have to be sensitive to the semantic category of the verb in the clause around which the negative is to be lowered. It would, thus, recapitulate the syntactic rule of negative raising right down to, and including, the information that *hope* exceptionally fails to allow negative movement. But the need for a negative-raising transformation is not obviated by the inclusion of the interpretive device of negative lowering, since the syntactic rule is still independently required for sentences like (38). Adopting the SM scheme, then, forces us to accept interpretive mechanisms that duplicate syntactic processes and, thus, fail to capture formally obvious generalizations about the language.

There are other peculiarities of queclaratives that the assumption of a semantic structure significantly different from surface structure can naturally explain. The behavior of polarity items (see Baker, 1970) is one such example. Polarity items are words or phrases that are sensitive to affirmativeness or negativeness of semantic context. Negative-polarity items occur mainly in grammatically negative contexts, and positive-polarity items in grammatically positive contexts. An example of the former is the phrase *a red cent*, with the meaning "any money at all." *Already* is a positive-polarity item in the speech of some, as the following examples show:

(48)   *I don't have a red cent.*
(49)   *I have a red cent.*
(50)   *John left already.*
(51)   *ᵈJohn didn't leave already.*

But in queclaratives, negative-polarity items appear only in **non-negative** contexts, and positive-polarity items only in superficially **negative** contexts.[4] The phrase *after all* is included in these sentences in order to isolate the queclarative interpretation.

---

[4] I am grateful to Jean Ehrenkranz LeGrand for calling these facts to my attention.

(52)   *After all, does Fred have a red cent?*
(53)   **After all, doesn't Fred have a red cent?*
(54)   *After all, didn't Jack leave already?*
(55)   *ᵈAfter all, did Jack leave already?*

This can be easily explained under the MM hypothesis, simply by claiming, as before, that the systematic semantic form of a queclarative has the opposite polarity of its surface form. This correlates well with the fact that it is semantic negativity that determines the occurrence of polarity items. Negatives from a semantic structure may fail to show up as overt negatives in surface structure for a variety of reasons, including coalescence with other predicates. In these cases, though, negative-polarity items still appear, and (for some speakers) positive polarity items are excluded.

(56)   *I doubt that he has a red cent.*
(57)   *He's too proud to ask for a red cent.*
(58)   *ᵈI doubt that he left already.*
(59)   *ᵈHe's too sleepy to leave already.*

In some cases, negative surface structures replace positive semantic structures, and in these cases positive-polarity items are allowed, but negative-polarity items are not. There is, for instance, a fairly common dialect of spoken American English in which the following two sentences are synonymous:

(60)   *I wouldn't be surprised if it isn't raining.*
(61)   *I wouldn't be surprised it's raining.*

In the dialect in which this negative-spreading rule is active, positive-polarity items can occur in superficially negative clauses. With a negative-polarity item in the *if* clause of a sentence like (60), only the semantically negative interpretation is available.

(62)   *I wouldn't be surprised if Jack hasn't left already.*
(63)   *I wouldn't be surprised if Jack didn't have a red cent.*

Thus, queclaratives behave quite like underlying assertions of opposite polarity, as far as the distribution of polarity items is concerned.

A proposal designed to prevent the unwanted duplication of effort I have outlined and, thus, save the SM hypothesis was made in a personal communication by G. Lakoff. Lakoff suggested that a transderivational constraint could take care of the facts concerning the use of queclaratives without recapitulating the independently needed rule of negative raising. Transderivational constraints are constraints

involving more than one derivation; as such, they are extremely powerful devices, which should be used with the utmost care. An in-
formal statement of the queclarative-interpreting rule making use of
a transderivational constraint is the following: A question can be interpreted as having the meaning of an assertion of opposite surface
polarity. More formally,

(64) $L_A \Vdash L_B$
if $L_A =$ S_0

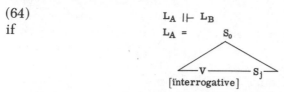

and there is a well-formed derivation from L_B:

where $L_B \ldots P_B \ldots S_B$
                                        $P_B =$ S_0

where $S_j = S_j$ in L_A.

The symbol "$\Vdash$" is to be read "conversationally entails." L_A and L_B
are semantic representations, P_B a derived structure, and S_B a surface
structure. The derivation from L_B to a structure containing a negative
in the highest clause may include negative raising or not. Thus, for
queclaratives containing negative-raising verbs, there will be two
derivations with logical structures entailed by the queclarative.

Such a scheme raises additional problems, however. Consider the
following queclarative:

(65)   *After all, did many arrows hit the target?*

The transderivational interpretive rule in (64) predicts that (65)
should have both the senses of (66) and (67), since in both cases
there is a negative in the highest clause:

(66)   *Not many arrows hit the target.*
(67)   *Many arrows didn't hit the target.*

For speakers for whom (66) and (67) ase distinct in meaning, (65) has
only the sense of (66).

The transformational treatment of queclaratives that is allowed
under the MM theory has no difficulty in handling these facts. The
senses (66) and (67) are distinguished at the level of sentence

meaning by the relative height of the negative predicate and the
quantifier *many* (see G. Lakoff, 1970d). Examples (68) and (69) are
highly simplified versions of the logical forms of (66) and (67),
respectively, which make explicit the underlying differences in
quantifier scope.

(68)

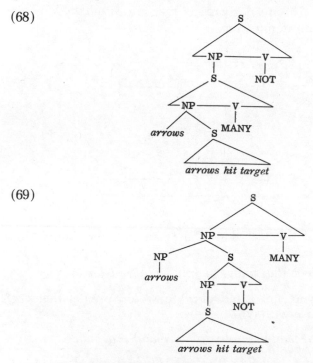

arrows hit target

(69)

arrows hit target

In the most widespread dialect of English, there is an independently needed derivational constraint forbidding derivations in
which a semantically asymmetric relationship between a quantifier
and a negative, such as that found in (68) and (69), gives rise to a
structure in which the opposite primacy relationships exist. The
semantically higher logical element must end up either higher in
surface structure or to the left of the semantically lower element.
Allowable derivations can be schematized as (70) and (71):

(70)

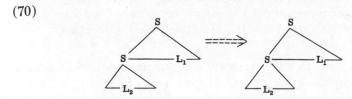

(71)

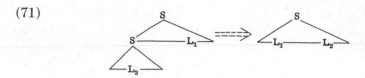

Examples (72) and (73) are derivations that are disallowed by the derivational constraint in question.

(72)

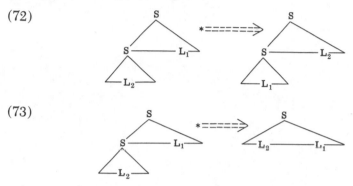

(73)

As an illustration of the fact that (72) is an improper derivation, consider the sentence

(74)   *I don't believe that many people own Studebakers.*

If derivation (72) were not ruled out, we would predict that (74) would share one sense with (75).

(75)   *I believe that many people do not own Studebakers.*

In the majority dialect, however (the one in which the derivational constraint under discussion is operable), (74) and (75) are distinct in meaning. Notice, also, that when the disappearance of a negative element is governed by a higher structure, the higher structure counts as the final position of the negative for the purpose of the derivational constraint. Thus, the following pairs of sentences are not synonymous in the majority dialect.

(76)   *I doubt that many arrows hit the target.*
(77)   *I think that many arrows didn't hit the target.*
(78)   *If many. arrows had hit the target, we would have won.*
(79)   *The fact that many arrows didn't hit the target caused us not to win.*

We can see, now, that the derivational constraint forbidding quantifier crossing predicts the correct senses for queclaratives that contain quantifiers, provided that queclaratives are derived transformationally from underlying structures containing a negative.[5] In particular, a semantic structure such as (69) can never become a queclarative. Such a derivation would involve the deletion of a negative on the basis of a structure higher than a higher quantifier, and this would violate the derivational constraint discussed earlier. The fact that a syntactic derivational constraint figures in the pairing of sense and form for queclaratives gives strong evidence in favor of the contention that the phenomena in question are, indeed, syntactic. I have no idea how the transderivational constraint (65) could be patched up so as to predict the unambiguity of (66). Somehow, a derivational constraint would have to be allowed to govern meaning entailments as well as derivations.

I also have a strong methodological objection to transderivational constraints such as (64), since the possibility of their existence entirely invalidates one of the standard sorts of arguments for underlying structure. The argument runs as follows: First, it is shown that there is a transformational process that depends for its application on some semantically relevant structural property. Next, it is shown that the same process affects sentences that share the same aspect of significance, but do not have the relevant structural property on the surface level. It is then concluded that the semantically relevant structure is present in the underlying syntacto-semantic representation of all sentences to which the syntactic rule applies. Note that all of the arguments for higher abstract clauses that were based on the distribution of spurious reflexives were of exactly this type. But if transderivational constraints exist that have the power of allowing syntactic rules to be sensitive to **entailed** sense, as well as to semantic content, then all such arguments fail. Take the case of the argument, presented in Chapter 2, based on the distribution of spurious reflexives after *like*. Instead of the conclusion that there is a syntactic conditioning factor involved in the case of apparently antecedentless first-person reflexives, transderivational constraints allow us the following explanation for these facts: First of all, there is an interpretive rule that states that nonperformative sentences are understood as though there were a higher performative clause:

[5] One case where both the transderivational constraint and the transformational treatment that I have suggested fall down has to do with the well-known ambiguity of the sentence *John doesn't beat his wife because he loves her.* Note that the corresponding queclarative *After all, does John beat his wife because he loves her?* is unambiguous. Both treatments discussed here predict that it should display both the meanings of the assertion.

(80)   L$_S$ $\vdash$

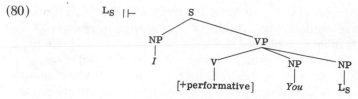

Next, there is a transderivational constraint that allows spurious reflexives to be created after *like* just in case the expression occurs in a semantic structure that entails a meaning form with a higher clause, the subject of which is coreferent with the object of *like*. Since any logical form entails itself, this constraint handles the cases where the antecedent is present as well.[6] Obviously, I must reject such modes of explanation, since this work is predicated on the validity of the performative analysis and the arguments for it.

There are numerous other criticisms that can be leveled at the theory that illocutionary force and surface form are closely allied, all based on the failure of this theory to distinguish truly indirect force from apparently indirect force. Many have been presented by Sadock (1972b) and Green (1972).

For one thing, the distribution of cooccurring items related to force is very difficult for the SM proposal to handle. I will consider only one illustrative example here. The word *please* in English has a very complicated range of uses. Let us restrict our attention here to the sentence adverb *please,* as opposed to the more-or-less free-standing item *please.* Sentence-adverbial *please* can precede a sentence without an intervening pause:

(81)   *Please don't handle the merchandise.*

and can occur sentence-internally:

(82)   *Passengers will please refrain from expectorating.*

or sentence-finally, preceded by a comma break in intonation:

(83)   *Pass the remoulade, please.*

Sentence-adverbial *please* often serves to soften explicit requests, or to render them more polite. But this is not always so. Its softening function has become so weak in the modern language that the following sentence does not clash stylistically:

---

[6] I should point out that not all transderivational constraints have the insidious characteristic of obscuring the distinction between the content of a sentence and what that content entails. In particular, some have been suggested (see G. Lakoff, 1970e) that affect one derivation on the basis of another that begins with the same semantic form. These seem quite innocuous.

(84)   *Please shut up.*

(See also the discussion of the mollifying function of whimperatives in Chapter 6.) Free-standing *please*, on the other hand, is a request all by itself. It is usually up to the addressee to figure out exactly what is being asked of him. However, it is usually a request to stop doing something (roughly speaking), or to undo something that has just been done. Sentence (85), for example, might be a request to close a window that has just been opened, to turn up the heat (which has just been turned down), or to cease ripping off the speaker's clothing.

(85)   *Please! It's cold in here.*

I doubt that (85) could be used dialogue-initially as a request for a blanket. At any rate, it is sentence-adverbial *please* that has interesting cooccurrence properties.

First of all, adverbial *please* can occur with imperative-form sentences that have the force of a request either pre-or postsententially:

(86)   *Please bring me a towel.*
(87)   *Bring me a towel, please.*

But it cannot occur with pseudoimperatives (see G. Lakoff, 1966)—sentences that have imperative form but do not have the force of requests:

(88)   **Take one more step, please, and I'll shoot.*
(89)   **To stop the boat, please head up into the wind.*
(90)   **Have a merry Christmas, please.*

In addition, sentence-adverbial *please* can occur with a range of sentences that do not have imperative form but can be used as requests. Certain surface questions with request force have this property; instead of sentence-initial *please*, these can have preverbal *please*. Notice that in imperative-form sentences, initial *please* is also preverbal. We can say, in general, then, that one of the normal positions for sentence-adverbial *please* is immediately preceding the verb whose fulfillment is being requested.

(91)   *Would you please remove your hat?*
(92)   *Can you move over, please?*

Gordon and Lakoff realized that the distribution of *please* was a problem for the SM theory that they propounded, and attempted to handle it in the following way: They claimed, as have others, that all questions are to be represented as requests, specifically requests for information, on the semantic level. As requests, they naturally allow sentence-adverbial *please*. The problems with this explanation are truly gargantuan.

First, *please* occurs with some nonquestions that are used as requests, as in example (82) and

(93)   *I'd like a package of Pall Malls, please.*

Second, there are many types of questions that can be used as indirect requests and with which *please* cannot occur.

(94)   **Don't you think you should please take out the garbage?*

(95)   **Don't you think you should take out the garbage, please?*

(96)   **Must you smoke, please?*

(97)   **Isn't it too cold in here, please?*

Third, this theory has no ability to explain the positions in which we find *please*. In the explicit requests for information that are supposed to correspond to whimperatives, *please* cannot be found immediately before the verb whose action is being requested in the corresponding whimperative. Compare (98) with (92).

(98)   **Tell me if you can please move over.*

Notice, also, that (99), which corresponds to the supposed source of (92) under Gordon and Lakoff's treatment, is not even a way of requesting the addressee to move over.

(99)   *Tell me if you can move over.*

According to Gordon and Lakoff's conversational postulates, both (92) and (99) should constitute requests, since they appear to share fundamentally the same semantic structure. It is, in fact, often the case that nearly synonymous sentences differ as to their potential use, and as to the cooccurrence properties that are associated with pragmatic function. A few examples should suffice.

(100a) *Can you please close the window?*

(100b) *Are you able to (*please) close the window?*

(101a) *Why don't you close the window?*

(101b) *How come you don't close the window?*

(101c) *What's the reason that you don't close the window?*

(102a) *Do you mind closing the window?*

(102b) *Are you opposed to closing the window?*

In each of these cases, only the (a) sentence is an indirect request for the addressee to close the window. It is, of course, unlikely that *can* and *be able, why, how come,* and *what's the reason that,* (see Zwicky and Zwicky, 1973) *mind,* and *be opposed to* are exact synonyms. What is important, though, is that they do share the salient meaning features that are supposed to be involved in their use as requests. Gordon and Lakoff account for the fact that sentences like (100a) can be used as requests by providing a general principle that requests can be gotten across by questioning the hearer-based sincerity conditions on requests (discussed earlier). For a speaker to request something sincerely, he must believe that the addressee is able to carry out the action. Thus, they claim, *can you do S* conversationally entails the force of *do S*. But the same prediction would erroneously be made for (100b) by parity of reasoning. The fact that apparently closely synonymous sentences can have radically different pragmatic values is an extremely grave problem for the SM theory.

Lest I appear too harsh on the theory of conversational postulates, let me reiterate that I am not arguing against them. I believe that a good deal of our ability to interact in conversation, and in other social contexts as well, must be explained in terms of a set of rules of behavioral inference such as those proposed by Grice and by Gordon and Lakoff. Indeed, my rejection of the UM thesis implies that parasyntactic devices are required to account for some cases of the use of sentences. What I am arguing against is the **strict** SM hypothesis, which claims that such rules are always involved when gross surface form and force fail to jibe.

The SM thesis also has strange things to say about language change. It would seem to imply that semantically encoded illocutionary force is extremely resistant to change, and perhaps even that it cannot change. I will consider an example from Israeli Hebrew.

As is probably the case in all languages, Hebrew has numerous standard ways of getting requests across. Of these, two are particularly interesting. One can use either a verbal stem plus gender and number suffixes:

(103a)   *ŠEV* ("sit!") (masc. sg.)
(103b)   *švu* ("sit!") (masc. pl.)

or a verbal stem with gender and number suffixes, as in (103), and a second-person prefix:

(104a)   *tešev* ("[you will] sit.") (masc. sg.)
(104b)   *tišvu* ("[you will] sit.") (masc. pl.)

The first form is used only as a request, while the second is also used as an indicative future, and is formed in the same way as the remainder of the indicative future forms—namely, with the aid of personal prefixes and gender and number suffixes. According to the SM theory, then, sentences using (a) forms would be represented as semantic requests, while sentences using (b) forms would be represented as semantic assertions. The significance of the second form, the SM theory claims, is conversationally entailed in the same way as the corresponding English sentence, *You will sit down,* entails an order or request.

Now, the first form is falling out of use, and for most verbs is never used at all in the spoken language. Yet it is not clear that, under the SM hypothesis, this development has any effect on the semantic representation of the **second** form. Even if the first form were to die entirely, the second form could still be looked upon as a semantic future declarative whose use as an imperative is a function of conversational entailment rather than of grammar. Statements from comparative grammars to the effect that, for example, the Slavic imperative reflects the old Indo-European optative (e.g., Meillet, 1965:329) would hardly make sense within the SM theory.

The actual situation is even more striking. The first form cannot be used in negative imperatives. Only the second form can:

(105)   *al sev
(106)   al tišev ("Do not sit.") (masc. sg.)

It should also be pointed out that the negative imperative is distinct from the negative future declarative, *lo tišev* ("You will not sit.") This fact, however, would not prevent a proponent of the SM theory from analyzing the monosignificant (106) as an underlying future declarative. As we have seen, Gordon and Lakoff provide mechanisms specifically for cases where, in their terms, the entailed force has an effect on the distribution of morphemes. Therefore, the SM theory both requires and allows sentences that are used as negative requests to be represented as future assertions. The strange consequence of this theory for the analysis of Modern Hebrew is the result that the language seems to lack logical structures with a negative predicate immediately under an imperative predicate.

But things are even worse. In a semantically based grammar such as Lakoff has advocated in much of his work, a verb like *šatak* ("keep quiet") would be assigned a semantic representation with a highest negative predicate, roughly: NOT (SPEAK $[x]$). Therefore, the imperative

(107)   *štok* ("Be quiet.")

would, after all, represent an instance of a semantic structure in which a negative predicate is immediately dominated by an abstract imperative predicate. Under the SM view, then, Modern Hebrew allows this semantic configuration just in case there is no direct reflex of the negative in surface structure. We are left with the almost Whorfian conclusion that a derivational constraint prevents speakers of Hebrew from constructing semantic structures with an imperative dominating a negative, except for the few cases where the negative can be incorporated into a single lexical verb.

These manifold absurdities can be avoided easily, and the facts of Modern Hebrew explained in a satisfying manner, by rejecting the SM thesis in favor of the MM proposal. Under a theory where the relationship between pragmatic meaning and form is not necessarily one-to-one, (104b) can be looked upon as the convergent surface form of semantic structures that differ in the nature of the higher abstract performative clauses that define illocutionary force. The lack of convergence in related forms, such as the negative, would therefore not be at all surprising.[7] The strange asymmetry among semantic forms that is claimed by the SM hypothesis to underlie sentences of Modern Hebrew would, furthermore, disappear. Example (106), as well as (107), would be a negative imperative, according to the MM view.

Another point that I wish to make against the SM theory of indirect speech acts concerns its implications for language comparison. The following are quite ordinary ways of getting across a request to open a door in Swedish, Hebrew, and Greenlandic. They are followed by rough morphemic translations.

(108)   *Tänk om Ni skulle opna doren.*
             ("Think whether you should open the door.")
(109)   *atá muxán liftóax et hadélet?*
             ("Are you ready to open the door?")
(110)   *matumik angmarniarit.*
             ("May you try to open the door.")

In all of these languages, distinct, unambiguous imperative forms

---

[7] This could be put more strongly. It is usually just this kind of partial convergence that ordinarily convinces us that we are dealing with linguistic ambiguity. Thus, to demonstrate that the verb *hang* is ambiguous between the two senses, "suspend" and "execute by suspending from a rope around the neck," it is sufficient to point out that, for example, the past-tense forms are distinct: *hung* and *hanged*, respectively.

exist for transmitting requests. Moreover, the particular morphemes and grammatical devices that distinguish these sentences from corresponding imperatives all have uses that resemble closely the uses of the literal translations just given. The SM theory would, therefore, require that the Swedish sentence be represented as a request to do some thinking, the Hebrew sentence as a question concerning preparedness, and the Greenlandic sentence as a wish of some strange kind. The SM theory would force us to conclude, in other words, that there is no particular difference in the **grammars** of English, Swedish, Hebrew, and Greenlandic that accounts for the fact that these literal translations are odd if used with the intent of getting someone to open a door. The important difference would reside in language-particular rules for the **use** of the language under the SM hypothesis. This result nullifies the most attractive feature of the SM theory: its claim that it can account for the facts surrounding indirect speech acts in terms of general principles of conversation. But in order for rules for the use of language to account for the differences that clearly exist among languages as far as what indirect speech acts are possible, the principles cannot be nearly as general as Gordon and Lakoff would hope.

Finally, I wish to call attention to the fact that, whereas conversational postulates and other natural-language rules of inference are necessarily transitive, the relationship among some indirect speech acts is not transitive. For example, Gordon and Lakoff provide, first, an equivalence between questions and requests for the addressee to tell the speaker something, and a conversational postulate that states that a question concerning the addressee's ability to do something can entail a request for him to do it—as in (11b) in this chapter. Since we must assume the validity of the following formulae for natural logic:

(111) $(A \equiv B \wedge B \Vdash C) \supset A \Vdash C$
(112) $(A \Vdash B \wedge B \equiv C) \supset A \Vdash C$

then the prediction is made that the following sentence entails a request to open the door, which it does not:

(113)   *Tell me if you can open the door.*

According to Gordon and Lakoff's treatment, (113) is the logical equivalent of (114):

(114)   *Can you open the door?*

And since conversational postulates are based on logical form, (113)

should also be the **conversational** equivalent of (114). This failure of
transitivity of supposedly logical laws could be due either to there
being a difference in logical form between questions and explicit
requests for information, or to there being a grammatical (rather than
a logical) source for the request understanding of sentences like
(114). I will argue in Chapter 6, in fact, that both of the specific proposals that combine to predict that (113) could be used as a request
are wrong.

The difficulties that arise from the SM hypothesis seem to me to be
every bit as insurmountable as those that surround the UM hypothesis. We are left, then, with the MM proposal, a theory that
offers no simple answer to the question of what the illocutionary
force of a sentence is. Under the MM hypothesis alone, we are
forced to search for subtler modes of determining what the semantically encoded speech-act value of an utterance is, rather than simply equating it with the sentence's use, or with its form. The aim of
the following chapter will be the development of criteria by which
we can tell which aspects of the use of a sentence are part of its
meaning.

5

Distinguishing Use from Meaning

In trying to decide which aspects of the pragmatics of a sentence are to be directly represented in semantic structure, it would be helpful to look again at the example of the Modern Hebrew imperative. As we have seen, it is reasonable to consider the form that looks like a second-person future declarative to be represented on the semantic level as a semantic imperative on one reading. But how did this state of affairs come about?

It is likely that future assertions can be used as suggestions for universal conversational reasons. To make a statement about a future volitional act of the addressee's, one must have reason to believe that the action will be carried out. Since one cannot, in fact, **know** such things, assertions about an addressee's future volitional acts can be construed as wishful speaking—that is, as requests, suggestions, or the like.

At some point in time, this use of second-person future indicatives in Hebrew became relexicalized, or better, resyntacticized, as a semantic request. I suggest that the development is rather similar to the change from metaphor to idiom. When an idiom such as, say, *down in the dumps* was spontaneously created by some linguistic innovator, it had only its literal sense. By rules of inference that are perhaps of a universal nature, the metaphorical values of the phrase could be arrived at. But the phrase eventually (or maybe very quickly—it makes no real difference) came to **mean** something that hitherto was only a metaphorical significance. The second-person future is, thus, a sort of speech-act idiom in Hebrew and should display the properties of an idiom. The principal difference between this idiom and others, as I see it, is that part of the disparity between its apparent meaning and its actual meaning involves the illocutionary force of the utterance. According to the abstract-performative hypothesis, illocutionary force is simply the part of the meaning of a sentence represented by the underlying performative clause. If other aspects of semantic structure can be idiosyncratically substituted for to form idioms, why not the performative clause as well?

I hypothesize that all indirect speech acts whose pragmatic specification differs from what the surface form appears to indicate arose when a frequently associated use became encoded in semantic form. This view explains why, for most indirect speech acts, there is a reasonable but indirect relationship between use and apparent sense. For example, it would be quite surprising if Hebrew displayed a third-person past-tense declarative as the universal realization of the imperative under certain circumstances. That is, it is not accidental that Hebrew does not have what looks like "He didn't close the door" for "Don't close the door." The reason is that "He didn't close the door" would hardly have been intended to imply "Don't close the door" often enough for that use to have become part of the meaning of the sentence. For similar reasons, it is not surprising that the idiom *down in the dumps* means "depressed" and that we do not use *in seventh heaven* or *on cloud nine* in this sense. The required derived metaphorical use was simply not available, and could therefore not become elevated to the status of meaning in these two cases. Yet from a **synchronic** point of view, there is no reason why these idioms should have exactly the senses they do, and not, say, the opposite senses.

Many sentences that can be used as requests look a lot like questions, and it is therefore tempting to call them "semantic questions," as the proponents of the SM hypothesis have. But, similarly, the verb *stick* in the sense of *adhere*, the verb *stick* in the sense of *pierce*, and the verb *stick* in the sense of *extend* all look alike right down to the fact that they all have the same strong preterite *stuck* and a homophonous past participle. Yet it would certainly be a mistake to explain this similarity within a synchronic grammar of English by claiming that there is a living relationship in their meanings. The relationship among these verbs is by now entirely historical, and leaves the language with a synchronic coincidence of a kind that has been, but should not be, a source of embarrassment to modern grammarians.

How can we tell, in the general case, whether a metaphor has become an idiom? How can we tell whether some aspect of the significance of a sentence is part of the meaning of the sentence, or whether it is entailed by the meaning or imposed by the context in which the sentence is uttered? In the case of indirect speech acts, how are we to know whether some aspect of the pragmatics of a sentence is encoded in its meaning, or whether it is a function of the use of the language? For nonpragmatic idioms, there seem to be formal criteria that allow a line to be drawn between them and metaphors, and, as I shall show, the class of indirect illocutionary acts can be divided into two groups on the same basis. There are sentences that have been termed "indirect speech acts" whose formal properties reflect their use, while there are others whose formal properties are just those we would expect from an examination of their surface form. The former, I maintain, are the sentences for which the SM hypothesis is wrong—that is, those whose meaning corresponds more closely to the use of the sentence rather than to its form. The latter are those for which the SM hypothesis is correct.

For convenience, I will group the formal properties that distinguish semantic sense from interpreted sense into three categories: cooccurrence properties, paraphrase properties, and grammatical properties.

It is intuitively plausible that these three kinds of distributional facts should distinguish meaning from use. From the inception of generative semantics, cooccurrence properties have been recognized as being correlated with meaning, and I will simply maintain that point of view in this work. It should come as no surprise to find out that the cooccurrence properties of idioms are correlated with their meaning rather than with their form. We should also expect idioms to be resistant to paraphrase, since the lexical items that comprise an idiom are not directly related to semantic structure and cannot therefore be replaced by lexical items that correspond in meaning to the meaning of their phonological twins. Neither should we be surprised to find that an idiom displays grammatical peculiarities vis-à-vis similar nonidiomatic expressions. In particular, it is reasonable to expect to find that an idiom is not subject to ordinary transformations. While the reasons for this are not entirely clear as far as formal grammar is concerned, one intriguing suggestion is made in Newmeyer (1972). This work claims that whether or not an idiom undergoes a transformational rule depends on whether or not the meaning of that idiom is structurally appropriate to the transformation. If Newmeyer's proposal is correct, then grammatical behavior can give us fairly direct insights into meaning. At any rate, idioms in general undergo relatively few transformations. It is also frequently the case that some otherwise optional transformation is obligatory for a certain idiom.

Let us compare, for illustrative purposes, the idiom *spill the beans* in its ordinary idiomatic sense of "to give away a secret," with an adaptation of a rather vivid metaphor of Donald Barthelme's (1967), *to put the red meat on the rug*, which can be used to signify something on the order of "to bring up an ugly subject." Let us compare these two superficially similar expressions with regard to the three sorts of formal properties mentioned earlier. In its idiomatic sense, *to spill the beans* does not allow any of the modifiers that we would ordinarily expect to cooccur with *beans* (e.g., *tasty, Lima, dried and shriveled,* etc.). There are, in fact, only a few adjectives that can modify *beans* in the idiom, principally *proverbial* and *ol'*. Notice, also, that with these adjectives, only the idiomatic sense is available. As far as verbal modifiers are concerned, only those that are appropriate to the meaning of the whole idiom are found. Thus, the following sentence is ungrammatical, since the adjective cooccurs only with the idiomatic sense and the adverb only with the literal sense:

(1)   *Bill clumsily spilled the proverbial beans.*

The idiomatic sense can cooccur with an indirect object because an indirect object is appropriate to the meaning of the idiom. The literal sense cannot take an indirect object, and sentence (2) is therefore ungrammatical:

(2)   *Bill spilled the beans, which were on sale at two cans for 29¢, to the cops.*

In short, the idiom has cooccurrence properties that reflect its meaning rather than its form.

By contrast, the metaphor *to put the red meat on the rug* can be metaphorical no matter what else occurs with it in the same sentence. The metaphor may become clumsy or strained or farfetched with the addition of material, but it can still be a metaphor. More important, nothing can cooccur with the metaphor which cannot occur with a similar phrase used nonmetaphorically. Although one can say

(3), example (4) is odd, even though the additional phrase fits the metaphorical significance.

(3)　　*He spilled the beans by mentioning Castro.*
(4)　　*?He put the red meat on the rug by mentioning Castro.*

Notice that attempts to paraphrase the idiom result in either a loss
of the idiomatic meaning or a rather low sort of humor. If there are
cooccurring elements that can occur only with the idiomatic sense,
sentences containing paraphrased idioms are less than grammatical.

(5)　　　　*?Ernest spilled the legumes to the cops.*
(6)　　　　*?Ernest dumped out the proverbial beans.*

The metaphor, however, remains intact when paraphrased, since
the metaphorical significance is derivative of the literal meaning, and
the meaning is preserved in an accurate paraphrase:

(7)　　　　*Denise placed the raw hamburger on the carpet.*

Among the miscellaneous grammatical phenomena that can affect
the construction *to spill the beans* in its literal sense, there are several that do not apply to the idiom (see Fraser, 1970). That is to say,
the literal sense can be isolated from the idiomatic sense by the
application of grammatical rules. One large class of grammatical
properties that idioms rarely display is the ability to be partially
reduced under formal identity with other sentential material, or to
act as antecedent in reduction transformations (but see Quang, 1971).
None of the following sentences has the idiomatic reading:

(8)　　*Ernest spilled the beans and Max, the chickpeas.*
(9)　　*Ferdinand bought the beans and Cedric spilled them.*
(10)　*The beans which Anita spilled were important.*

The active metaphor, on the other hand, has the property of being
extendable by the addition of reduced or reducing material. For example, it is necessary to interpret both conjuncts of sentences (11)
and (12) either metaphorically or literally, but the metaphorical
sense is not necessarily lost. Sentence (12) might indicate that an
ugly subject was raised and then squelched.

(11)　*Sri put the red meat on the rug and Kali, the oatmeal on
　　　the tablecloth.*
(12)　*Sri put the red meat on the rug and Kali ate it.*

Besides reduction rules, the idiom undergoes numerous other
productive transformations only reluctantly, if at all:

(13)   ??*What Eric spilled was the beans.*
(14)   ??*It was the beans that Dorothy spilled.*
(15)   ??*The beans were spilled to the FBI by Giulio.*
(16)   ??*The beans were believed by John to have been spilled by Bill.*

However, grammatical transformations have little effect on the metaphor, except, perhaps, to deprive it of some of its poetry:

(17)   *What Eric put on the rug was the red meat.*
(18)   *It was the red meat that Dorothy put on the rug.*
(19)   *The red meat was put on the rug by Giulio.*
(20)   *The red meat was believed by John to have been put on the rug by Bill.*

The fact that semantic distinctness is correlated with formal features of sentences makes the hypothesized parallelism between non-pragmatic idioms and indirect speech acts more than just an analogy. It is now an empirically testable hypothesis, since the analogy could fail in several ways. The claim that the MM hypothesis makes is that some indirect speech acts — but not all of them — will be characterized by exactly the kinds of formal features that characterize lexical meaning. Some, that is, will behave as idioms, and the rest as metaphors. Moreover, it ought to be the case that sentences that show formal reflexes of the speech act for which they are used, rather than of the speech act that their surface form seems to represent, will be those that are felt to mean what they **do** rather than what they **say**. It could happen, then, that all indirect speech acts — or none of them — turn out to display formal features related to their use. In either case, the MM hypothesis and the hypothesis that there are always formal reflexes of meaning would be falsified. It could also turn out that a dichotomy among indirect speech acts based on the presence or absence of formal features would disagree wildly with our intuitions concerning meaning. I will show that the analogy does not fail in any of these ways, and thus gives us the ability to tell which aspects of the use of a sentence are encoded in its semantic representation, and which are not. The cooccurrence, paraphrase, and grammatical behavior tests that I have outlined have been, in fact, the basis of numerous arguments within generative grammar and, more particularly, within generative semantics. The thrust of these arguments was that a certain set of sentences were characterized by a systematic ambiguity that should be displayed on the underlying syntactic level (see Zwicky, to appear). It is difficult to imagine what sort of progress generative semantics would have made were it not for the assumption that formal properties mirrored meaning. Yet there are certain dangers involved in these tests that we must be wary of.

In using cooccurring material to isolate a supposed sense of some construction, one must be reasonably assured that the cooccurring material does not itself have the very meaning that the argument is designed to show the rest of the sentence as having. For instance, it would not do to argue that *John played the piano* is ambiguous between a habitual and an event sense (even though it is) on the basis of the fact that *John habitually played the piano* is unambiguous. This sort of reasoning would allow one to conclude that *John is wearing suspenders* is ambiguous between a red-suspender sense and a non-red-suspender sense because of the fact that *John is wearing red suspenders* is consistent with only one of these interpretations.

The danger in using grammatical processes to argue for aspects of meaning lies in using the same aspect of meaning to argue for the existence of the grammatical process in the first place. Suppose one desired to demonstrate that *Bill drove to Columbus* is ambiguous between a sense that indicates that Bill stopped at the outskirts of the city and one that means that he drove into the city. It could be argued that there is a syntactic rule that deletes prepositions that stand before the preposition *to*. But it is only in case this rule is independently motivated that the existence of the unambiguous sentences *Bill drove up to Columbus* and *Bill drove into Columbus* points to an ambiguity in the original sentence.

Finally, in using paraphrase phenomena to argue for idiomatic status, one must be sure that the relevant part of the meaning of the supposedly idiomatic construction is captured by the paraphrase.

Let us now train these methodological guns on the problem of distinguishing pragmatic meaning from conversationally entailed pragmatic significance. In Chapter 3, some evidence was presented in support of the contention that example sentence (27) of that chapter—repeated here as (21)—was to be regarded as having a highest performative clause containing the verb *inform* at the level of semantic structure. Two sorts of formal arguments were presented there, one based on cooccurrence and another on grammatical peculiarities. We can now see that (21) shows the third kind of formal property, which indicates that its meaning and surface form differ considerably. Not every paraphrase of the relevant parts of (21) succeeds in conveying its original force. Compare (21) with (22):

(21)   *We regret to inform you that your policy has been can-
        celed.*
(22)   *We *lament/? are disturbed/?are chagrined (etc.) to in-
        form you that your policy has been canceled.*

Let us turn now to more difficult examples. Consider sentences
(23) and (24):

(23)   *Will you close the door?*
(24)   *When will you close the door?*

Both sentences can be used to get the addressee to close a door. Both
sentences appear to be questions. Nevertheless, there is a fairly
strongly felt difference between (23) and (24). Sentence (23) rather
bluntly **tells** someone to close a door, while (24) only **hints** at it. This
intuitive feeling is confirmed by the fact that (23) displays the formal
properties that we should expect of a semantic imperative, while (24)
does not.

Sentence (23), for example, can take a sentence-adverbial *please* or
kindly immediately before the verb that describes the action being
requested, but this will not work in (24):

(25)   *Will you please/kindly close the door?*
(26)   **When will you please/kindly close the door?*

Another element that characteristically occurs in imperatives is an
indefinite vocative (Thorne, 1966):

(27)   **You're six years old, someone.*
(28)   **Are you six years old, someone?*
(29)   *Get me a beer, someone.*

This indefinite vocative can occur in (23) (despite the second-person
subject), but not in (24):

(30)   *Will you close the door, someone?*
(31)   **When are you going to close the door, someone?*

It might seem that the element *please* contains the request sense, but
this does not strike me as correct. If it did, we should expect such
implied requests as (32) to be grammatical with *please*.

(32)   *Wouldn't it be a good idea to (*please) close the door?*

At any rate, it is quite impossible to claim that the indefinite vocative
someone has the meaning of a request, so at the very least, the
monosignificance of (30) argues for an underlying request sense.

There are certain idiomatic predicates that occur principally in imperatives:

(33)   *Buzz/Flake off.*
(34)   **Bill buzzed/flaked off.*
(35)   **Who just buzzed/flaked off?*

These expressions can also occur in sentences of the form of (23), but not in sentences of the form of (24).

(36)   *Will you buzz off?*
(37)   *Buzz off, will you?*
(38)   *?When will you buzz off?*

Reason-for-speech-act adverbials typical of requests can occur with (23), but not with (24):

(39)   *Since I've got my hands full, will you close the door?*
(40)   *?Since I've got my hands full, when are you going to close the door?*

Sentences like (23) are rife with grammatical idiosyncrasies, while those like (24) do not display any that I know of. For example, (23) can have an unmotivated conditional verb form:

(41)   *Would you close the door?*

There is no need to assume an antecedent for what appears to be a questioned consequent in (41), as there is for (42), the corresponding version of (24):

(42)   *When would you close the door?*

Thus, example (41) can appropriately initiate a discourse, but (42) cannot.

"Whimperatives," as I have called sentences like (23), are transformationally related to a form that has been called a tag imperative (see Katz and Postal, 1964). For each grammatical sentence of the form

$$(43) \frac{\text{MODAL (SUBJUNCTIVE) (NEGATIVE)}}{1} \frac{you \ (please)}{2} \frac{\text{VP}}{3}$$

there is a sentence of similar force with the order of constituents 3, 1, 2. The only modals that are found in sentences of the canonical form (43) are *can* and *will*:

(44) $* \left\{ \begin{array}{l} Should \\ May \\ Might \\ etc. \end{array} \right\}$ *you please close the door?*

Similarly, only the modals *can* and *will* show up in tag imperatives.

(45)   *Close the door, $\begin{bmatrix} should \\ may \\ might \\ etc. \end{bmatrix}$ you?

In the majority dialect, the morphemes SUBJUNCTIVE and NEGA-TIVE are mutually exclusive; that is, the canonical form for whimperatives for most speakers contains the expression $\begin{Bmatrix} SUBJUNCTIVE \\ NEGATIVE \end{Bmatrix}$. Strings like (46) do not occur for most speakers.

(46)   ^d*Couldn't/wouldn't you please close the door?*

And in this dialect, tag imperatives must also have one or the other, but not both, of the morphemes SUBJUNCTIVE and NEGATIVE. Sentence (47) is ungrammatical in the majority dialect.

(47)   ^d*Close the door, wouldn't/couldn't you?*

But there are speakers who find (46) grammatical. The fact that the same speakers also accept (47) is evidence of the strongest sort in favor of a transformational relationship between whimperatives and tag imperatives.

I have called the rule responsible for the relationship between whimperatives and so-called tag imperatives **fracturing**, and re-dubbed tag imperatives **fractured whimperatives** (Sadock, 1970). Some light is shed on the details of the rule of fracturing by the following data: In some dialects, (48) represents a grammatical sentence form, but (49) does not:

(48)   ^d*Don't make so much noise, will/would you?*
(49)   **Don't make so much noise, won't/wouldn't you?*

Note that there is no grammatical source structure from which (48) could stem by simple transposition of the modal and the subject:

(50)   **Will you don't make so much noise?*

However, there is still something to be gained by relating (48) to a grammatical whimperative—namely, (51).

(51)   *Will you **not** make so much noise?*

If this relationship is made explicit, the fact that negative tags are forbidden when the imperative itself is negative would need no special comment in the grammar. That prediction would spring automatically from the fact that all sentences like (52) are ungrammatical.

(52)   *Won't/wouldn't you **not** make so much noise, please?

In order to produce sentences like (48), then, fracturing will have to affect a structure like (51), resulting in an intermediate stage roughly like (53).

(53)

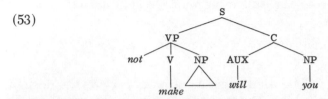

The rule responsible for the appearance of *do*[1] would have to apply subsequently to the production of intermediate structures like (53) and, *a fortiori*, after the rule of fracturing. Now, notice that fracturing applies only to question-form sentences that have a request sense. Since (54) is unambiguously a request, the rule must be sensitive to this aspect of significance, and we can conclude that the request significance of the question-form sentence is an aspect of meaning.

(54)   *Close the door, will you?*

The passivized congener of (23) loses its straightforward request sense, and, indeed, ceases to exhibit the cooccurrence properties of a request. The same holds for the cleft sentence. But the ability of (24) to be used to get someone to close a door is not diminished by these transformations. Thus, these transformations must also be sensitive to whether or not sentences of the form of (23) are requests, but are indifferent to the intended use of sentences like (24).

(55)   *Will the door be (*please) closed by you?*
(56)   *Will it be you who (*please) closes the door?*

---

[1] In earlier generative grammars, *do* arose in questions, negatives, and so on through the agency of a *do*-insertion (or support) transformation (see, for example, Chomsky, 1957). Recently, however, it has been suggested that the *do*'s that appear are semantically relevant, and what is really going on is that, in the cases complementary to where *do* support was thought to operate, a *do*-deletion rule applies. There are facts surrounding the appearance of *do* in fractured whimperatives, and imperatives in general, that argue strongly against the theory that *do* is present in just the right places in semantic structure. In negative imperatives and fractured whimperatives, *do* is found with all varieties of the verb *be*, whereas the same semantic predicates do not take *do* in negative questions:

(a)   *Don't be a fool.*
(b)   **Doesn't John be a fool?*

Certainly, semantic *do* cannot be distributed in just this way.

(57)   *Will it be the door which you (*please) close?*
(58)   *When will the door be closed by you?*
(59)   *When will it be you who closes the door?*
(60)   *When will it be the door which you close?*

Finally, paraphrase can isolate the request and question sense of (23) but not of (24).

(61)   *Are you going to (*please) close the door?*
(62)   *When are you going to close the door?*

Example (61) can still be used to get a person to perform the desired act, but the inability of this sentence to take sentence-internal *please* demonstrates that it does not have the **sense** of a request.

We see, then, that just as distributional facts are capable of distinguishing idiom from metaphor, they are capable of distinguishing encoded force from use or effect. In the instance we have examined, the results of applying these formal criteria square with intuition. We perceive, as speakers of English, that (23)—despite its surface form—is a request on one reading—in other words, that it is actually ambiguous between a request sense and a question sense.

There has been one formal test described in the literature for distinguishing ambiguity from vagueness. This is George Lakoff's well-known conjunction test (G. Lakoff, 1970a). Lakoff maintained that part of what is required for deletion under identity between conjuncts is identity of meaning. Thus,

(63)   *Bill is standing on the bank and so is Sam.*

has only two senses and not four. Both men are standing either on the margin of a river or on top of a financial institution, but (63) cannot mean that, say, Bill is standing at the edge of the Mississippi and Sam on top of the First National. *Bank* in one sense cannot reduce *bank* in the other sense.

But this reduction-under-identity test fails to discriminate between idiom and metaphor (see Zwicky and Sadock, 1973). That the test fails in this case is not surprising. It does not really make sense to speak of an expression's being **vague** between a literal and a metaphorical interpretation. Vagueness is a matter of lack of specification of meaning. But metaphors, by definition, have the literal meaning. One cannot further specify the meaning of a metaphorical expression in such a way as to guarantee that it has a metaphorical interpretation.

The reduction test gives rather strange results when applied to metaphors. Consider the following sentence:

(64)   *Phyllis wants to live in Hoboken and so does Everett.*

Suppose the first clause is used metaphorically to convey something like *Phyllis has poor taste.* For most speakers, it is then impossible to interpret the reduced second clause literally. That is, (64) cannot have an interpretation like *Phyllis has poor taste and Everett wants to live in Hoboken.* But many speakers find it possible to interpret the first conjunct literally and the second conjunct metaphorically. Lakoff's test for ambiguity, thus, gives ambiguous results when applied to metaphor.

The reduction test also gives peculiar results with regard to certain fairly obviously nonillocutionary pragmatic aspects of language use. Jokes, insults, and hyperboles all behave very much like metaphors as far as reduceability is concerned. This **crossed sense** is found only if the literal conjunct is first. A sentence like

(65)   *Mark Spitz has a moustache and so does your mother.*

can be understood as a literal statement followed by a nonliteral insult. But sentence (66), where the first conjunct is to be understood nonliterally, is quite strange:

(66)   ??*Your mother has a moustache and so does Mark Spitz.*

Now, notice that a conjunction of whimperatives, one of which is reduced, has only two pragmatic interpretations, and not four. Both halves of (67) can be meant as questions, or both as requests, but the mixed understandings do not occur:

(67)   *Will you take out the garbage and will you do so before
         I get home?*

For sentences like (24), reduction under identity gives exactly the same peculiar results that we saw in regard to metaphors. Sentence (68) has **three** significances—a doubly literal one, a doubly snide one, and a sense in which the first conjunct is taken literally and the second as a left-handed request. The other crossed sense is peculiar.

(68)   *When will you take out the garbage, Sid, and when will
         you do so, Andy?*

Despite their problems, reduction tests are syntactically based and will be used, along with other syntactic tests, as a definition of sentence meaning. In particular, such tests will be applied in the next chapter in investigating the aspect of meaning called "illocutionary force."

6

Some Covert Illocutionary Acts in English

INTERROGATIVE SENTENCES

In this chapter, I will more or less randomly present some of the results achieved by using the formal criteria outlined in the previous chapter. My principal aim has been to discover what the range of nonexplicitly represented illocutionary force in English is. The various illocutionary types that I shall discuss form, without a doubt, only a small fraction of the total number. I have chosen to use gross surface form as an organizing principle, and shall restrict my attention to sentences with the surface earmarks of questions in this section, and those of interrogatives in the next.

We have already seen that there are formal properties that indicate that sentences of the form

(1) $\left\{\begin{matrix} Will \\ Can \end{matrix}\right\} \left\{\begin{matrix} \text{SUBJUNCTIVE} \\ \text{NEGATIVE} \end{matrix}\right\}$ you $V_{[-\text{stative}]}X$

should be considered to be ambiguous between a request and a

111

question sense. That is, two different deep structures (at least) underlie sentences of the form of (1), one with an abstract verb of requesting, and the other with an abstract verb of questioning in the semantic performative clause. The formal properties that distinguish the request sense are in complementary distribution with the formal facts characteristic of the question sense.

Consider, for example, the class of unambiguous requests formed by fracturing whimperatives. These cannot cooccur with clauses that call into doubt the felicity conditions on questions:

(2)   *Take out the garbage, will you, or don't you know?*

Fractured whimperatives cannot take the question-softening adverb *by any chance:*

(3)   *Take out the garbage, by any chance, will you?*
(4)   *Take out the garbage, will you, by any chance?*

True questions allow the pretag *tell me,* but these requests do not:

(5)   *Tell me, take out the garbage, will you?*

True questions are conjoinable only with a subsequent question, apparently because questions by their nature demand a response in order for the dialogue in which they are found to proceed properly:

(6)   *Do you have any relatives in the USSR and I'll wash the dishes.*
(7)   *Do you have any relatives in the USSR and are you a member of the VFW?*

But whimperatives, including those that have undergone fracturing, can be followed by conjoined nonquestions:

(8)   *Take out the garbage, will you? and I'll wash the dishes.*

It might be claimed that the sense of these cooccurring elements is simply incompatible with an intention of requesting. It is easy to see, though, that this is not the case. Thus, (9) can be **used** to request a particular book from a librarian,

(9)   *Do you have* **Les Philosophes de la Boudoire,** *or don't you know?*

sentence (10) can be **intended** as a request for a match,

(10)   *Do you have a match, by any chance?*

and (11) can be uttered for the purpose of getting someone to close a window, turn up the heat, bring a blanket, or the like.

(11)   *Tell me, is it cold in here?*

The ill-formedness of examples (2)–(5) must therefore be a function of the grammar of English. Similarly, sentence (12) can entail a request for a drink, but cannot be followed by a conjoined nonquestion, as shown by the ungrammaticalness of (13). Thus, the well-formedness of (8) is also a grammatical fact.

(12)   *Do you have anything to drink?*
(13)   **Do you have anything to drink? and I'll make the sandwiches.*

What distinguishes the members of the pairs (2) and (9), (3)—or (4)—and (10), (5) and (11), and (8) and (13) is that in each pair, the first is a semantic request while the second is a semantic question. The first, that is, has the sense of a request; the second only conveys one.

While whimperatives show many of the formal properties of requests, they also differ from requests in certain respects. As Green (1972) has pointed out, whimperatives require a verbal response whether or not they are carried out, and certain responses that constitute assents to whimperatives are not well-formed assents to imperative requests. It is possible to agree to carry out a whimperative-form request by answering *Yes*, but this is quite an odd response to an imperative-form request. Both whimperative and imperative requests can be reported using the verb *ask*, as in *He asked me to get off his toe*, but only imperatives can be reported with the verb *tell*, as in *He told me to get off his toe*.

There is also a difference between these two kinds of requests as to what can be (and has been) loosely called "politeness." It is sometimes said that whimperatives are more polite than imperatives. I think, though, that this is a serious misapprehension of the situation. There are certain requests that, by their nature, are rude. If whimperatives were polite forms, then rude requests in whimperative form ought to display an internal stylistic clash. But I find no such clash in sentences like

(14)   *Shut up, would you?*
(15)   *Will you cut it out?*
(16)   *Get off my back, won't you?*

whereas certain other deferential forms do display an incompatibility with rude requests:

(17)   *?I humbly request that you shut up/cut it out/get off my back.*

Thus, whatever is involved in the difference between whimperatives and imperatives does not directly have to do with politeness. It seems to me that, rather than it being the case that whimperatives are polite, imperatives **cannot** be polite. Nor do I think that the discourteousness of imperatives is part of their meaning. I would guess, instead, that there are culture-specific rules of the use of language that tell us that it is uncivil directly to request something of a social equal or superior. Yet we have seen that whimperatives function and pattern quite like requests, and that there is good reason to consider them to **be** requests. To accommodate these various facts, I suggest (without a great deal of confidence) that the indirectness of whimperatives be explicitly made a part of their meaning—that is to say, that the abstract performative clause underlying whimperatives be taken to be roughly paraphrasable as *I indirectly request of you* . . . .

Let us turn next to another sort of question-form sentence used to get an addressee to do something. Green (1972) has examined sentences like

(18)   *Why don't you put a record on?*

It is clear that these must derive from two semantic sources, one of which has a question sense and one of which has what she has termed an **impositive** sense. An impositive sentence is, roughly, one by means of whose illocutionary force the speaker indicates that he wishes to impose his will upon the addressee. The class thus includes (besides requests) orders, demands, suggestions, and so on. The impositive sense of (18) is subject to two special transformational rules: fracturing and *you* + TENSE deletion. The application of these rules results in sentences like (19) and (20), respectively.

(19)   *Put on a record, why don't you?*
(20)   *Why not put on a record?*

The interrogative pronoun is not paraphrasable in the impositive sense, although it is in the question. Thus, (21) does not have an impositive sense, and (22) and (23) are ungrammatical.

(21)   *For what reason don't you close the door?*
(22)   **Close the door, for what reason don't you.*
(23)   **For what reason not close the door?*

Finally, *why don't you* impositives do not display the cooccurrence properties of questions. Sentence (24) is not a normal sentence to use in getting someone to close a door, although, of course, it can succeed in doing this for perlocutionary reasons. Sentences (25) and (26) are not well-formed.

(24)   *Why don't you close the door, or don't you know?*
(25)   **Close the door, why don't you, or don't you know?*
(26)   **Why not close the door, or don't you know?*

And in contrast to true questions, *why not* impositives can all take a subsequent nonquestion conjunct:

(27)   *Close the door, why don't you, and I'll close the windows.*

Now, there is a similar class of sentences represented by (28).[1] But there are glaring asymmetries between *why not* impositives, which suggest the positive action, and *why* impositives, such as (28), which suggest nonaction.

(28)   *Why paint your house purple?*

If (28) were precisely parallel to (20), then it should have as its source a structure like that of (29), just as (20) was related to (18).

(29)   *Why do you paint the house purple?*

But (29) differs quite strikingly in sense from (28). Moreover, (29) is not subject to fracturing:

(30)   **Paint the house purple, why do you?*

While I have no explanatory treatment for this discrepancy, the facts can be accommodated fairly easily. We need to assume that derivations beginning with a semantic impositive pass through an intermediate stage resembling (29), and that this is obligatorily converted into structures like (28). The *you* +TENSE deletion rule will, in other words, be optional in the presence of a negative morpheme, and obligatory otherwise. Note, also, that this deletion rule and fracturing are incompatible anyway. Thus, (31) is ungrammatical.

(31)   **Paint the house, why not?*

The most straightforward way of handling this fact is to order the deletion rule before fracturing. Then, if the deletion rule applies, it will remove a part of the structural description of the fracturing rule and render it inapplicable. Given these admittedly ad hoc assumptions, the ungrammaticalness of (30) is accounted for.

[1] For a discussion of this class of sentences from the point of view of conversational postulates, see Gordon and Lakoff (1971).

At any rate, *why* impositives, both positive and negative, show all of the kinds of formal traits that point to their semantic distinctness from their interrogative *Doppelgängers*. We must, therefore, now concern ourselves with the identity of their nonquestion illocutionary force. While they belong in the intuitive class of impositives, it is clear that they do not behave quite like requests of imperative form. That is to say, they are not whimperatives. *Why* impositives are not very happy with sentence-adverbial *please* or *kindly*, especially if they have undergone either fracturing or *you* + TENSE deletion;

(32)   *Why don't you ?please/?? kindly take out the garbage?*
(33)   *Why don't you take out the garbage, please?*
(34)   *Why not *please/*kindly take out the garbage?*
(35)   *Take out the garbage, why don't you, *?please?*

Green has noticed that *why* impositives require somewhat different responses from those required by whimperatives and imperatives. One can assent to any of these by responding *OK, Sure, All right,* and so on. To demur, one can respond to an imperative or whimperative with *No*, but this is an inappropriate response to a *why* impositive:

(36)   A. *Why not take out the garbage?*
                 B. **No.*

Unlike requests and whimperatives, *why* impositives may take an inclusive first-person plural subject:

(37)   *Why don't we treat ourselves to a malt?*
(38)   *Why not treat ourselves to a malt?*

Compare

(39)   **Won't we please go to the movies?*

Fractured *why* impositives with first-person plural subjects do not exist as such:

(40)   **Go to the movies, why don't we?*

But we do find sentences with the expected sense and the expected tag, like the following:

(41)   *Let's go to the movies, why don't we?*

These have no apparent unfractured source, as the ungrammaticalness of (42) shows.

(42)   **Why don't we let's go to the movies?*

We can fill the lacuna in the paradigm formed by the lack of a straightforward fractured first-person *why not* impositive, and at the same time provide a source for peculiar sentences like (42), by identifying (42) as the fractured version of (43).

(43)   *Why don't we go to the movies?*

I do not mean to imply that (43) is the **source** of (42), but only that (42) and (43) are transformationally related—that they share a common derivational ancestor.

Costa (1972) has pointed out the existence of a very similar paradigm:

(44)   *Shouldn't we buy a boat?*
(45)   **Shouldn't we let's buy a boat?*
(46)   *Let's buy a boat, shouldn't we?*
(47)   **Buy a boat, shouldn't we?*

Again, I suggest that the skewed paradigm can be regularized by providing (44) and (46) with a common derivational source.

Note that there is a strong similarity between the forces of sentences like (43) and (44). This similarity is reflected by the fact that these sentences have similar cooccurrence properties. As with *why not* impositives, *shouldn't* impositives occur either with first-person plural subjects, as in (44), or with second-person subjects:

(48)   *Shouldn't you drive slower?*

Like the corresponding impositives in *why not*, these do not freely occur with *please*.

(49)   *??Shouldn't you drive slower, please?*

Yet (48) is not really a question, which is another property it shares with *why not* impositives, as may be seen from the fact that it may be followed by conjoined nonquestions.

(50)   *Shouldn't you drive slower, and I suggest you keep both hands on the wheel, too.*

And fractured *shouldn't* questions do not take speech-act adverbials typical of questions:

(51)   **Let's solve this problem first, shouldn't we? or don't you know?*

Thus, *shouldn't* and *why not* impositives are neither semantic questions nor semantic requests.

Notice that *shouldn't* and *why not* impositives are mutually conjoinable, and that when they have first-person plural subjects, each is
conjoinable with simple impositives beginning with *let's*.

(52)   *Why not paint the house purple, and shouldn't you
        make the shutters chartreuse, too?*
(53)   *Shouldn't you paint the house purple, and why not
        make the shutters chartreuse, too?*
(54)   *Shouldn't we see a skin flick tonight, and let's invite
        Kirk, too.*
(55)   *Why don't we see a skin flick tonight, and let's invite
        Kirk, too.*

Two other question-form impositives that share numerous of the
properties of *shouldn't* and *why not* sentences are those in *how
about* (or *how's about*),[2] and those in *what do you say* or *what say*.
Some examples are the following:

(56)   *How's about treating ourselves to a malt, and let's in-
        vite the Grimeses, too.*
(57)   *What (do you) say you take out the garbage, and why
        not check the mailbox while you're at it?*

Because all of these are also conjoinable with a succeeding explicitly performative suggestion (cf. example (50), I propose that they
all be treated as having an abstract predicate like, or identical with,
the verb *suggest* in the underlying performative clause. This leaves a
great deal of syntactic adjustment to be done by the syntactic component in an apparently ad hoc manner. The contracted form *let's*,

[2] An interesting property of sentences of the form *How about* NP? is that the action
that is being suggested is not explicitly mentioned in the sentence. There appear to be
two ways for this ellipsis to take place: First, an intersentence deletion rule of the
kind described by Morgan (1972) can be involved, as in this dialogue:

(a)   *Who shall we blame this analysis on?*
(b)   *How about Sam?*

But sentences of this form can also be used to initiate a dialogue. In such a case, as
far as I can tell, there is only one verb that we understand as having been deleted—
namely, *have* in the sense of *consume*. Thus, *How about a beer?* can mean something
like "How about your having a beer?" (as when a bartender says it to a customer) or
"How about our [inclusive] having a beer?" (as when I say it to a colleague). The two
bases for the deletion in these sentences explain why the following dialogue is good if
the first speaker is a waiter and the second a customer, but bad if the first speaker is
the customer and the second the waiter:

(c)   X: *How about a beer?*
                                   Y: *OK, how about a beer?*

for example, will, under this treatment, have nothing semantically in common with the verb *let*. It will be idiomatically inserted partially on the basis of the nature of the abstract performative clause. The fact that it resembles a literal structure whose sense is such that it **entails** a suggestion will, as with other similar facts concerning idioms, be treated as a diachronic fact, and will not be mentioned at all in a synchronic grammar of English.

There are, indeed, several idiosyncratic properties of suggestions in *let's* and the other types of suggestions discussed here. There is, for one thing, the special reduction of the second-person pronoun (if, indeed, it should be called a pronoun in a synchronic grammar; cf. *ᵈlet's us*), and the peculiar form *don't let's*, which has idiosyncratically had the negative element raised (Costa, 1972). These oddities strengthen the hypothesis that this *let's* is idiomatic in these sentences.

The numerous details of the relationship among these idiosyncratic sentences, which I claim are all semantic suggestions, will be left entirely uninvestigated. There may well be a good deal of regularity in their patternings; but if I am right in saying that they are speech-act idioms, we should not be surprised to find a good deal of irregularity as well.

To conclude this discussion of the surface manifestations of suggestions, I shall summarize the test properties by which, I suggest, they may be recognized.

They are impositives and can be assented to by answering *OK, Sure, All right*, and the like, but can be refused only by responding with *No* (or the like) and a reason for the dissent. This is a property of explicit suggestions as well:

(58)   ARTHUR: *I suggest that we drop the subject.*
         JACK: *No.

but

         JACK: *No, I don't think we should.*

Next, the subject of the clause expressing suggested action can be either a second-person or a first-person plural noun phrase. While this is sometimes not true as far as the surface form of explicit suggestions is concerned, it is a valid observation for semantic structure. A sentence like *I suggest that Bill take out the garbage* must be interpreted very much like *I suggest that we see to it that Bill takes out the garbage*. The same thing can be said for apparent counterexamples among indirect suggestions. *How about Bill taking out the garbage* means something like *How about our/your letting/making Bill take out the garbage.*

And last, suggestions can take the postsentential tag *OK?*

None of these tests is, by itself, a sufficient reason for adjudging a sentence a semantic suggestion. It is possible, though, that only semantic suggestions display all of these properties.

I will turn my attention next to the oft-quoted hypothesis that questions are semantically requests for information (see, for example, Gordon and Lakoff, 1971). The claim is that there is no special abstract performative verb in the underlying performative clause that accounts for the illocutionary force of questions, but rather that there is a semantically complex higher abstract structure approximately like structure (59):

(59)

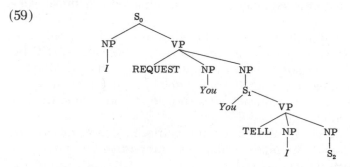

Here, REQUEST is the abstract performative verb found in, for example, true imperatives, and TELL is the abstract performative verb that occurs in the logical form of assertions. TELL does not, of course, function performatively in this structure, since it is in an embedded clause. Only S_2 will surface directly, although the higher structure will have its effect on the surface form of S_2.

I will argue, on the basis of the formal properties of question-form sentences, that this hypothesis is sometimes true. Most sentences with the surface shape of questions will be seen, in fact, to be ambiguous between a request sense, for which an underlying structure like (59) is appropriate, and a more basic question sense, for which it is not. The latter sense should probably be represented as having an underlying atomic verb of asking.

The theory that questions are a type of request receives support from the fact that, under appropriate circumstances, most questions can take a postsentential *please*, which, as we have seen, is an ordinary property of semantic requests. A teacher might ask,

(60)   *Johnny, who discovered the Bronx, please?*

and a census taker might be caught saying something like

(61)   *How many children do you have, please?*

There are circumstances, however, where the use of *please* with interrogatives is inappropriate. The teacher who uttered (60), for example, would hardly say,

(62)   *? Johnny, do you have to go to the bathroom, please?*

and it would be unlikely for the census taker to say,

(63)   *? Where did you get that lovely dress, please?*

Operating under a formal theory of linguistic pragmatics, such as the one advocated in this book, makes it necessary to determine whether the difference in acceptability in the given context between sentences (60) and (62), or (61) and (63), is a matter of meaning. The inappropriateness of a given sentence to a given context is surely sometimes a matter of sentence meaning, but just as surely sometimes not. The sentence *Feed the cat* is inappropriate if the intended referent of the definite noun phrase is a dog. Here, the inappropriateness of the sentence is related to the lexical meaning of the noun *cat*. On the other hand, a sentence like *I was born under the sign of Cancer* might be inappropriate if spoken to a patient with a malignant tumor. It is hard to believe, though, that this fact has anything to do with the **meaning** of the sentence. It is not immediately obvious, however, whether the inappropriateness of questions like (62) and (63) in ordinary contexts is a matter of meaning, and, hence, grammar, for it is possible to invent contexts, as outlandish as they may be, in which either is appropriate. Suppose that a pharmaceutical house has come up with a new product, **Micturex,** which is reputed to be a wonder diuretic. Suppose, also, that the drug has been administered to an entire fifth-grade class. Miss Jones is supposed to indicate on a chart which pupils have been affected in the hoped-for way. When she gets to Johnny, she could properly utter (62).

Note that the salient difference between this situation and the more ordinary situations under which (62) is odd is that here the teacher is not personally interested in the information conveyed by the response. She is interested in **how** the query is answered, rather than in **what** is answered. Similarly, in the cases where (60) and (61) are appropriate, the asker has no personal stake in the response. Teachers presumably know the answer to test questions, and census takers presumably do not take a personal interest in the facts they gather. There are numerous formal facts reflective of this difference. Hence, I conclude that the representation of the meaning of a question must include some specification of whether the question is asked for the purpose of enlightening the speaker or not.

Besides sentence-adverbial *please*, there are other adverb-like items that differentiate questions to which one wants to know the answer from those to which one wants merely to hear the answer. There are a number of prepositional phrases like *in the world, in the hell*, and several saltier cousins that in one common dialect can follow interrogative pronouns just in case the speaker is interested in the further specification of that noun phrase.[3] I should mention that there is a second use of the same range of items that indicates exasperation. We can focus our attention on the distribution of the former type simply by considering questions asked for the first time in a dialogue. The first time the teacher poses the question, she cannot ask,

(64)   ?*Where in the world did Columbus set sail from?*

nor could the census taker ask as part of the survey,

(65)   ?*Where in the world does your husband work?*

but the teacher could say,

(66)   *Johnny, what in the world have you got in your mouth?*

and the census taker could be reasonably expected to ask, for her own edification,

(67)   *Where in the world did you get that lovely dress?*

Notice that *wh— in the —-* and *please* are mutually exclusive in questions. The following sentence, as far as I can tell, is never appropriate as a first inquiry.

(68)   **Where in the world did you get that lovely dress, please?*

As I have pointed out, it is only the extraordinary questions, those asked without personal interest in the answer, that allow the usual marker of requests, *please*. For this reason, I have dubbed such queries **requestions**, and proposed that these—and only these—be identified as semantic requests (Sadock, 1972b).

---

[3] I am grateful to Rudolf de Rijk for calling my attention to the interesting distributional properties of these phrases.

Requestions and questions differ sharply in grammatical properties. In particular, there are several special syntactic rules to which requestions, but not questions, are subject. Requestions, uniquely, can be formed by simple deletion of the asked-for noun phrase:

(69)   *The discoverer of Hispanola was?*
(70)   *Your previous address was?*

Alternative requestions can be formed without a conjunction, whereas questions cannot. These have question-final intonation on all but the last disjunct:

(71)   *Was Michelangelo born in France, Italy, or Puerto Rico?*
(72)   *Was your income for the past year less than $500, $5,000 to $15,000, more than $15,000?*

It is difficult to find examples where paraphrasability distinguishes between requestions and questions, principally because of the fact that there is at most one morpheme in a question that is crucially involved in signaling its force. In asking quiz questions, however, one can substitute a demonstrative for an interrogative phrase. The following sentence could be used on a quiz show, for example, with the same force as the question *What ungainly-looking bird is the symbol of Louisiana?*

(73)   *This ungainly-looking bird is the symbol of Louisiana.*

Notice that sentences like (73) are appropriate only as test questions, and not, for example, when information is being gathered, even though that information is not for the asker's benefit. The reason is obvious. To use a demonstrative correctly, a speaker must know its referent. If he knows the identity of a noun phrase whose specification he is requesting from an addressee, he must be administering a test. Thus, while test and survey questions comprise a natural class of requests for vocal response, they differ in important ways. Far too little is known about the more detailed properties of test and survey requestions for me to venture a guess as to their logical structure.

It is now possible to note and to explain the fact that sentences (74), (75), and (76) are three ways ambiguous, two ways ambiguous, and unambiguous, respectively.

(74)   *Can you close the window?*
(75)   *Can you close the window, please?*
(76)   *Can you please close the window?*

Sentence (74) might be (a) a question aimed at enlightening the speaker, (b) a survey requestion (asked of, say, an arthritic), or (c) a whimperative request for the addressee to close a window. Sentence (75) can have only force (b) and (c), and (76), only force (c). The occurrence of *please* in (75) removes one of the senses, since the information question is not a request. *Please* can precede the main verb in the clause that is the direct object of a verb of requesting. For some speakers, the matrix verb need not be a performative.

(77)   *Bill asked me to please not hang around the play-
          ground.*

There is an optional rule that shifts *please* to the end of its clause. In certain dialects, this rule is restricted to cases where the verb of requesting is abstract:

(78)   *Please don't offer candy to children.*
(79)   *Don't offer candy to children, please.*
(80)   *Bill asked me not to offer candy to children, please.*

Thus, (75) is ambiguous. The final *please* can have originated in a clause whose main verb is (abstract) TELL, or in the clause whose main verb is *close*. Sentence (76) is unambiguous, since *please* can occur before a verb only if that verb is the main verb of the object clause of a verb of requesting.

A cautionary note: Requestions can be used for questions, and questions can be used for requestions. The teacher who says,

(81)   *Now what in the world is seven times six?*

is posing a true question for didactic reasons. We should expect a requestion here, but find, instead, an unambiguous information question. Rather than weakening the arguments for the semantic difference between these two types of queries, occurrence of questions for requestions adds some more evidence, for such occurrences always convey a special hypocrisy that is adequately captured by the analysis. The teacher who utters (81) is pretending not to know the answer to his or her question.

Similarly, when the country club manager says to the new applicant,

(82)   *What is your name, please?*

he is purposely giving the impression that the answer is unimportant to him, that he doesn't really want to **know** the name but simply needs it for the records. Again, his mendacity can be made explicit in a formal theory that recognizes the difference between questions and requestions.

Let us examine next sentences of question form that commit their utterers to the opposite view from what is apparently asked. These "queclaratives," as I have called them, distinguish themselves in a great many ways from genuine inquiries.

As I have pointed out elsewhere, queclaratives allow polarity items characteristic of the proposition that the speaker is committed to the truth of. With the negative-polarity item *a damn thing* we find the pattern

(83)   *Who knows a damn thing about syntax?*
(84)   *Nobody knows a damn thing about syntax.*
(85)   **Somebody knows a damn thing about syntax.*

and with the positive-polarity item *pretty (adjective)*, the pattern

(86)   *Who isn't pretty good at giveaway chess?*
(87)   *Everyone is pretty good at giveaway chess.*
(88)   **Someone isn't pretty good at giveaway chess.*

Queclaratives do not allow phrases, such as *by any chance* or *wh---in the ----*, that signal information questions:

(89)   ?*Does Arthur, by any chance, know a damn thing about syntax?*

(90)   ?*After all, who in the hell has a clue about that?*

Queclaratives allow subsequent nonquestion conjuncts:

(91)   *After all, isn't Chicago a beautiful city (?) and besides, it's got thirteen Mandarin restaurants.*

There are grammatical peculiarities that differentiate between queclaratives and true questions. True questions are usually signaled by the inverse order of the subject and first auxiliary constituent. I have put it neutrally because of the fairly widely accepted hypothesis of McCawley's (1970a) that the question reflects the underlying order of constituents, and that a rule is required to produce the subject-verb-object order characteristic of declarative sentences. At any rate, information questions can also be found with subject-verb-object word order, but queclaratives cannot.

(92)   *Bill lent money to who(m)?* (question)
(93)   *Who did Bill ever loan money to?* (queclarative)
(94)   **Bill ever lent money to who(m)?*

In some dialects, queclaratives can be reduced all the way to nonrestrictive relative clauses, while for true questions, the reduction stops at the point of parenthetical conjuncts:

(95) ᵈ*Symbolic logic, which who cares about anyway, is awfully tough.*

(96) **Symbolic logic, which by the way who invented (?), isn't my cup of Postum.*

(97) *Symbolic logic—and by the way who invented it?—isn't my cup of Postum.*

Since queclaratives are formally distinct from questions, they must differ in underlying structure from questions.

Before attempting to decide just what the underlying representation of queclaratives is, I wish to examine another question-like sentence type, the so-called "tag question." The canonical form of tag questions is

(98) $\text{NP}_i \text{ AUXILIARY} \begin{Bmatrix} \phi \\ \text{NEGATIVE} \end{Bmatrix}_1 \text{X,}$

$$\text{AUXILIARY} \begin{Bmatrix} \text{NEGATIVE} \\ \phi \end{Bmatrix}_1 \text{PRO}_i$$

Sentences of this form are quite characteristic of English, and occur regularly in few other languages. Strings of this form can be read with two distinct intonation patterns, each of which receives a distinct interpretation. With question intonation on the tag, the sentence is a question, but it is simultaneously an expression of a previously held assumption, of which the speaker is no longer fully sure. One might utter

(99)   *There is no present king of France, is thére?*

if he thought he knew something about modern Europe, but had just overheard a conversation between two philosophers in which the present king of France was continually mentioned. The utterer of (99) will not be particularly surprised, no matter which answer he receives. He will also, in all likelihood, not be particularly satisfied with a simple *Yes* or *No*. The speaker would appreciate some explanation for his confusion—for example, an excuse for his having held an erroneous belief

(100)   *Yes, but he lives in Cicero and drives a truck.*

or an account of the events that caused him to lose faith in his cherished notion:

(101) *No, we philosophers just prefer to talk about nonexistent things.*

I suggest that tag questions of this sort be assigned a logical structure that explicitly includes the speaker's assumption, in addition to the question he is posing. Structure (102) is an approximation of this logical form:

(102)

```
                              S
            ┌─────────────────┼─────────────────┐
          S_0               AND               S_0'
      ┌────┴────┐                         ┌────┴────┐
     NP        VP                        NP        VP
      │    ┌────┼────┐                    │    ┌────┼────┐
      I    V   NP   NP                    I    V   NP   NP
           │   │    │                         │   │    │
        INFORM You  S_1                      ASK You   S_1'
                 ┌──┴──┐                            ┌──┴──┐
                NP     VP                          NP     V
                 │   ┌─┴──┐                         │     │
                 I   V    NP                       S_2   TRUE
                     │    │
                  ASSUME  S_2
```

Several, but by no means all, of the details of this tentative structure can be motivated syntactically and semantically. First of all, notice that the obligatory polarity difference between the base and the tag that shows up in surface structure is not present at all in the proposed representation of the meaning of this kind of tag question. This hypothesis is supported by not inconsiderable evidence that points to the superficiality of this polarity reversal. Tags occur that would be ungrammatical as whole sentences. Consider example (103):

(103)　　　*Sam didn't leave until three o'clock, did he?*

The tag in this sentence cannot arise from a whole sentence by the application of a tag-reduction rule (as in Stockwell, Schachter, and Partee, 1973), for this supposed source is ungrammatical:

(104)　　　**Did Sam leave until three o'clock?*

Next, the polarity of the tag depends crucially on the transformational history of the base sentence. If it so happens that at the level of surface structure, an overt negative is found in the highest clause of the base, none appears in the tag; and if, for whatever reason, there is no negative in the highest surface clause, then one appears in the tag. Each of the following pairs has tags of opposite polarity, despite the synonymy of the sentences in each pair.

(105a) *You don't believe that transformations change meaning, do you?*

(105b) *You believe that transformations don't change meaning, don't you?*

(106a) *No one is likely to win,* $\begin{cases} ^{d}are\ they? \\ ^{d}is\ he? \end{cases}$

(106b) *It's likely that no one will win isn't it?*

(107a) *Cynthia likes few men, doesn't she?*

(107b) *Cynthia doesn't like many men, does she?*

(108a) *Phil is unable to play Couperin, isn't he?*

(108b) *Phil isn't able to play Couperin, is he?*

Negative raising is responsible for the ultimate position of the negative in (105a), while the rule of subject raising has applied in (106a), and special lexical-insertion rules that substitute single lexical items for multiple predicates have obscured the negative in (107a) and (108a).

Moreover, it is clear that the whole shape of the tag is governed by the surface shape of the base.[4] In the following sentence, the subject of the base, a copy of which is found in the tag, is believed not to be present at all in semantic structure, but rather to be inserted by the syntactic rule of *there* insertion:

(109)   *There are two capitals of Bolivia, aren't there?*

---

[4] Actually, I am oversimplifying here, since the shape of the tag is not **completely** dependent on the surface form of the base. I know of the following sorts of counterexamples to the most simple-minded account of tag formation. First, strongly negative adverbs in the main clause of the base can count as a negative element and produce a positive tag:

(a)   *Duncan scarcely ate anything, did he?*
(b)   *Cynthia seldom lies, does she?*

but

                    Cynthia infrequently lies, $\begin{cases} ^{*}does\ she \\ ^{?}doesn't\ she \end{cases}?$

In order to count as a main-clause negative, the adverb must be positioned in front of the verb:

(d)   *Cynthia lies seldom,* $\begin{cases} ^{*}does\ she \\ doesn't\ she \end{cases}?$

Related to these facts (apparently) is the fact that many speakers find (107a) and its

In example (110), the surface subject arises through the operation of the passive transformation.

(110)   *Your nose was bobbed, wasn't it?*

These and numerous similar facts all indicate the superficial nature of the form of the tag. The theory of the meaning of tag questions embodied in structure (102) makes the claim that the form of the tag is superficial in two ways. It does not contain anything that could account for the polarity of the tag vis-à-vis the base, and it includes a question different from the apparent source of the surface question. The postulation of underlying structures such as (102), therefore, makes necessary the assumption of a rule of tag formation. If this rule is cyclic, and ordered toward the end of the cycle, it will correctly produce the required surface tags. The formulation of the rule is quite straightforward, and will not be gone into here.

Another group of facts that support the analysis of tag questions suggested here concerns such sentences as (111) and (112). These have been discussed in R. Lakoff (1969a).

(111)   *I don't suppose you're bored, are you?*
(112)   *I guess it's stopped raining, hasn't it?*

In these cases, the tag is formed, not on the basis of the highest surface clause of the base, but rather on the basis of the complement clause. Sentence (111) appears to have the form of the tag based on the complement, and the polarity based on the polarity of the highest clause. As Lakoff shows, though, the negative has been raised from the complement clause. Thus, the tag-formation rule can apply before this raising, and, in fact, would have to if the rule is to be cyclic; and the correct specification of the polarity of the tag arises automatically.

Lakoff attempted to give a uniform treatment of tag questions by claiming that the clauses with *suppose* and *guess* in (111) and (112) are performative clauses. The only difference, then, between (112) and the following sentence, in her treatment, would be that the optional rule of performative deletion has applied in the case of the latter.

---

positive-tag analogue unacceptable.

I know of one case where the auxiliary in the tag does not mirror the auxiliary structure of the base. Many people find the following sentence quite grammatical:

(e)   *Bill has got two Cadillacs, doesn't he?*

Compare

(f)   *°Does Bill have got two Cadillacs?*

(113)   *It's stopped raining, hasn't it?*

She analyzed both as stemming from the same underlying structure, one having a highest performative clause of supposing.

There are quite a few difficulties with this analysis, most of which are circumvented by assuming a more complicated semantic structure along the lines of (102). At the same time, the principal advantage of Lakoff's scheme, the fact that it permits a uniform description of tag questions such as (112) and the more usual variety exemplified by (113), is retained. Lakoff's analysis gets into trouble first over the fact that *suppose, guess, assume,* and the like are not performative verbs when used with the sense that they have in tag complements. *Guess* has a performative sense much like that of the verb *estimate:*

(114)   *I hereby guess that there are three hundred twenty-nine jelly beans in the bowl.*

Suppose and *assume* have similar performative senses in sentences like

(115)   *I assume, for simplicity's sake, that π is equal to 3.*
(116)   *We suppose, for the sake of the discussion, that all mice are equal in IQ.*

Notice that none of these sentences can take a complement tag. The sense of *guess, suppose,* and *assume* is very different in the cases just given from the sense of these verbs that is relevant to the study of tag questions.

In addition to the fact that the base cannot take *hereby* in tag complement sentences,

(117)   **I hereby guess it's raining, isn't it?*

such sentences distinguish themselves from explicit performatives in not being reportable in the same way. An instance of (112), for example, cannot be accurately reported by, say,

(118)   *Aard guessed that it was raining.*

The performative use of *guess* can, of course, be described in this way. Sentence (119) can be an earnest account of an instance of (114):

(119)   *Jimmy guessed that there were three hundred twenty-nine jelly beans in the bowl.*

Structure (102) avoids identifying the real or abstract *assume (suppose, guess)* clause as the performative clause by embedding it as the complement of a higher performative clause. I have supplied the actual performative clause with a verb different from that found in assertions because it does not seem appropriate to consider such self-descriptive statements as *I believe . . . , I suppose . . .* , and so on as assertions. Note the oddity of sentences like the following:

(120)   [?]*I claim that I assume that it is raining.*

I believe, in fact, that most declarative-form sentences are ambiguous between an assertive sense and an informative sense, but I am not in a position to justify this belief at present.[5]

A final criticism of Lakoff's proposal is its inability to account for the fact that the sort of tag questions under consideration here really are — or at least include — questions. The formal indication of this is the fact that the cooccurrence properties of questions and of tag questions with question intonation are alike. They may be followed only by conjoined questions, since they demand an answer:

(121) *It's not raining, is it* (?) **and get me a cigarette/**and it's supposed to be nice tomorrow.*

They demand, as a felicity condition, that the speaker assume that the addressee has the knowledge to answer:

(122) *It's six o'clock, isn't it* (?) *or aren't you wearing a watch?*

The speaker may not simultaneously profess to have the asked-for information and felicitously utter a tag question of this kind.

(123) **Stickball is an Olympic event, isn't it, which I've known for a long time.*

Finally, tag questions concerning knowledge available only to the speaker are odd, just as questions are:

(124)   [?]*I'm tired,* $\left\{ \begin{matrix} am\ I\ not \\ ^{d}aren't\ I \end{matrix} \right\}$?

(125)   [?]*Am I tired?*

The questionness of tag questions is captured by postulating semantic structures for them along the lines of (102).

An obvious drawback to postulating very abstract complex logical structures like (102) as the form underlying tag questions is that this

---

[5] The distinction between the two types of declaratives corresponds closely to Kimball's (1970) distinction between reportive and expressive sentences.

necessitates writing a fairly powerful transformation that builds surface tags without taking into account the underlying form of the tag.
We should rightfully ask why English should include such an unusual, apparently perverse rule in its grammar. How did this rule arise?
In order to answer these questions, let us return our attention to the
fact that English is unusual in having tag questions of the form it
does. Most languages, perhaps all, have sentence types with the
pragmatic significance of English tag questions. In many cases, indeed, such sentences take the form of a declarative sentence plus a
tag. In several languages, such tags differ from English tags in that
they are invariable: The same tag suffices for all declarative-form
sentences. Frequent examples of such tags can be translated as *yes?*,
no?, *right?*, *true?*, *is it true?*, *not?*, *is it?*, *isn't it?* English, in fact, has
a few of these alongside of opposite-polarity tags. The nonnegative
ones are reasonably close to the semantic form postulated in (102), so
that otherwise-needed grammatical processes suffice to yield sentence (126) from an appropriately filled-in semantic structure of the
form of (102).

(126)   *It's raining, right?*

Now, notice that in the following sentence, the tag could either be
an opposite-polarity tag or a fixed tag in a dialect (such as Indian
English) that has a fixed tag *isn't it?*

(127)   *It's raining, isn't it?*

Perhaps the English opposite-polarity tags arose from fixed tags
through overgeneralization from sentences like (127). This is especially possible (I hesitate to say likely) in a language, such as
English, that has frequent occurrences of *it* as the subject of a sentence from impersonal constructions, and the rule of extraposition
besides occurrences of the real pronoun.

To summarize my thinking on tag questions in English with question intonation on the tag: They all stem from semantic structures indicating an assumption and a question about the addressee's opinion
of the truth of this assumption. The performative verb in the first
conjunct contains a factive-complement performative verb such as *inform*. These semantic structures may be realized in a number of
ways. Tag formation, a fairly superficial rule, may replicate part of
the complement clause, and reverse the polarity of the tag. The
clause containing ASSUME may be either deleted or realized with
the verbs *assume*, *guess*, or *suppose*, and finally, the tag may be
deleted altogether.

The other intonation pattern for tag questions has high stress and pitch on the auxiliary verb in the tag, and rather low stress on the pronoun. The tag has approximately the same intonation as the imperative *Kiss me.*

With this stress, the tag question has a very different force. The utterer of (99) who uses nonquestion intonation on the tag is firmly convinced of the accuracy of the proposition expressed by the base. But he demands, in the tag, a statement of agreement from the addressee. Such sentences are commonly used as steps in verbal arguments.

These two tag-question types differ sharply in formal properties other than intonation. The one with question intonation allows the ordinary mark of (positive) information questions, *by any chance*, to be associated with the (negative) base. Without question intonation on the tag, *by any chance* is ungrammatical in the base.

(128) *There aren't any two-horned unicorns, by any chance,*
        àre thére/*áre thère?

With question intonation, felicity-condition modifiers appropriate to questions are found, but not otherwise.

(129) *Linguists make lousy spouses, dòn't théy/*dón't thèy,*
        or don't you know?

A negative base may contain strict negative-polarity items only if the tag has nonquestion intonation:

(130) *There isn't a thin dime in the treasury, *is thére?/is*
        there.

With nonquestion intonation, a tag sentence may be followed by a conjoined nonquestion:

(131) *It's raining, *isn't it/?isn't it, and it'll probably rain*
        tomorrow, too.

Finally, tag questions with falling intonation on the tag form nonrestrictive relative clauses more readily than those with rising intonation:

(132) *Cigarettes, which you smoke, dón't yòu/?dón't yòu,*
        decrease intelligence in rats.

The perspicacious reader will have noticed that the formal properties that distinguish tag questions with rising intonation from those with falling intonation are just those that distinguish true questions from queclaratives. In particular, the unexpected properties of queclaratives are shared by tag questions with falling intonation. The

parallel between true questions and tag questions with rising intonation is complicated by other factors, but I shall return to that problem
shortly.

I propose, then, that the two types of tag questions be assigned
more or less radically different logical structures reflective of their
pragmatic difference, on the basis of the fact that they display different formal properties. In addition, I propose that queclaratives
and tag questions with falling intonation on the tag be assigned similar logical structures. This proposal stems from the extreme similarity
of their formal behavior, as well as, of course, their similar force.

In Sadock (1971), it was suggested that the underlying structure of
queclaratives be taken to be very much like the most immediate
predecessor structure of tag questions—that is, an assertion and a
subsequent question of opposite polarity. The tag question with
falling intonation was assigned the same structure in that paper. Sentences (113) and (134) would both have been assigned a structure on
the order of (135) under this analysis.

(133)   *Isn't Danish beautiful?*
(134)   *Danish is beautiful, isn't it?*
(135)

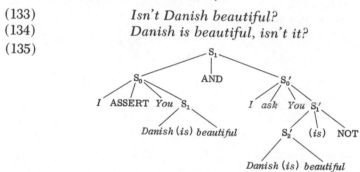

There are several serious difficulties with this proposal, not the
least of which is that the hypothesized semantic form is contradictory. It is also the case that structure (135) misses the semantic mark
by a good distance. Queclaratives and the corresponding falling-
stress tag questions commit a speaker absolutely to the proposition
expressed by the base of the tag question. But a sequence of an assertion followed by a question of opposite polarity concerning the
same proposition implies great uncertainty on the speaker's part.
Compare (133) with (136), in which the second sentence is to be
taken as a serious question à la structure (135).

(136)   *Danish is beautiful. Isn't Danish beautiful?*

Yet another fact over which the proposal embodied in (135) comes
to grief is that tag questions such as we find in English are only

sparsely found among the world's languages. But the proposed deep structure is very close to the surface structure of the English form. Why, then, would the vast majority of the world's languages go so far out of their way to disguise what is being said? Since English is the unusual language in this case, it is far more likely that it represents the deviant example, the case where a relatively unexpected process is involved in the relationship between meaning and form. Another difficulty still is the fact that, unlike the situation that obtains in the case of an assertion, the utterer of a queclarative or falling-stress tag question presumes that the addressee shares the same opinion. To felicitously assert something, one must assume that his addressee is **unaware** of or does **not** believe what is being asserted. One demonstration of the nonassertiveness of tag questions and queclaratives is their inability to cooccur with the pseudo-conditional tag *if you can believe such a thing* (see Weiser, 1973). *Such a thing*, in this expression, as Weiser shows, can refer only to asserted propositions:

(137) *Bill bought a Cadillac, if you can believe such a thing.*

(138) **Did Bill buy a Cadillac, if you can believe such a thing?*

(139) **Buy a Cadillac, if you can believe such a thing.*

(140) **Bill bought a Cadillac, if you can believe such a thing, didn't he.*

(141) **After all, didn't Bill buy a Cadillac, if you can believe such a thing?*

Note the contrasting behavior of the assertion, example (137), and the tag question and queclarative, examples (140) and (141), respectively. Thus, both tag questions with falling intonation and queclaratives fail to show the properties either of the questions or of the assertions that would be predicted on the basis of hypothesized underlying structure (135). I have no particularly clear idea, however, of what the common semantic source for queclaratives and falling-stress tag questions ought to be. Figure (142) represents a sheer guess with no syntactic backing.

Note that tag questions with rising intonation are also matched in sense by one sense of simple interrogative sentences. Thus, sentences like *Don't chickens lay eggs?* are ambiguous between a queclarative sense and a sense like that of a tag question with question intonation. A nonnegative interrogative form is, then, at least four ways ambiguous. A sentence like *Do roosters lay eggs?* can be used to ask a question when the speaker has no preconceptions as to the

(142)

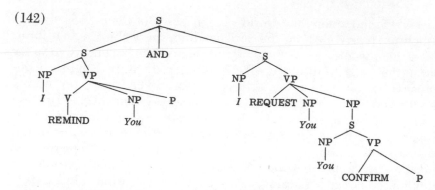

answer (simple question), when he does not care about the answer (requestion), in the case where the speaker felt that the proposition was false but now has reason to doubt his feeling (incredulous question), or to remind the addressee of the fact that both he and the speaker believe the proposition to be false (queclarative).

One idea for specifying the syntactic relationship that the two semantically distinct types of tag questions display is the following. Suppose that the underlying semantic structures that represent the two sorts of tag questions converge at an intermediate stage of derivation, through the application of the tag-formation rule, in a structure like the tag question, but with an unreduced tag—in other words, a structure like (143).

(143)

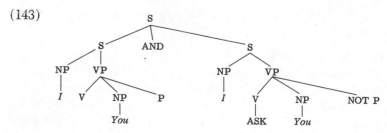

From this intermediate structure, the tag question would arise through the application of the rule of verb-phrase deletion, which is independently motivated. Verb-phrase deletion is needed to account for the synonymy of such pairs as (144) and (145).

(144)   *Arthur eats brie, but does Niels eat brie?*
(145)   *Arthur eats brie, but does Niels?*

The derivation of the corresponding interrogative forms would require a new rule of base deletion. This rule would have to be written in such a way as to wipe out the intonational distinction between the two types of tag questions. In other words, the intonation of the tag in both kinds of tag questions is determined by the performative verb in the semantic structure of the tag, but in queclaratives, it is the syntactically introduced ASK in (143) that governs the intonation.[6]

Besides these quasi-regular formations, there are numerous constructions with a more restricted domain that have the surface form of questions, but either a nonquestion illocutionary force or the illocutionary force of a different question. An example of the latter kind occurs in *Alice in Wonderland* (Carroll, 1960:265). Humpty Dumpty is speaking:

> "So here's a question for you. How old did you say you were?"
> Alice made a short calculation, and said, "Seven years and six months."
> "Wrong..." Humpty Dumpty exclaimed triumphantly. "You never said a word like it..."
> "I thought you meant 'How old *are* you?'" Alice explained.
> "If I'd meant that, I'd have said it," said Humpty Dumpty.

Alice had good reason for thinking that Humpty meant "How old **are** you?." If the question had been, "How old did you inform me you were?" Alice might not have been so easily fooled. The interpretation is, thus, sensitive to paraphrase. For many speakers, the question must also be interpreted literally—that is, as a question about what was said, if the complementizer is not deleted.

(146)   *How old did you say that you were?*

Ordinarily, questions can be gotten across by imperatives in *tell me;* for example, (147) and (148) have similar speech-act values.

(147)   *What are you eating?*
(148)   *Tell me what you're eating.*

But an imperative like (149) is approximately equivalent only to a question about what was said. Alice could not have been mislead by it.

(149)   *Tell me how old you said you were.*

---

[6] Two fairly serious difficulties with this scheme are that it does not account for interrogative-word queclaratives, such as *Who wouldn't want to live in Pittsburgh?*, and that it does not account for the fact that opposite-polarity questions very often have just the two senses they have in English in languages that lack opposite-polarity tag questions. It is possible that the queclarative and incredulous-question senses are more or less naturally derivable on the basis of conversational postulates. It this is so in general, then English has grammaticized this otherwise conversationally entailed significance, one of the manifestations of the grammaticization being the relationship between interrogative-form sentences and tag questions.

Since the effect of questions can also be accomplished with requests in *tell me,* and since requests can occur in the question form that I have called a "whimperative," we should expect doubly indirect questions to occur. This expectation is fulfilled by sentences like (150).

(150)   *Could you tell me how old you are?*

An interesting form for asking something indirectly is one that appears to be a question concerning the addressee's knowledge. Sentence (151) could be (and most likely would be) used to ask about the outcome of an election, but it could also be used to ask only whether the addressee has the knowledge of the outcome of the election:

(151)   *Do you know who won the election?*

Notice that a *tell me* imperative does not capture the indirect sense of this question:

(152)   *Tell me whether you know who won the election.*

In addition, not all paraphrases of *know* can be used to ask something indirectly. Example (153), for instance, is either a literal question or a sort of reminder, but not a request for the time.

(153)   *Are you aware of what time it is?*

Sentence (151) can also be a reminder, and, as if this triple ambiguity were not enough, it can have a fourth pragmatic value. A common use of sentences like (151) is to set the addressee up for some surprising information. This use and the use as an indirect question are often confused in actual conversation. Misunderstandings exemplified by (154) and (155) are amazingly common:

(154)   A: *Do you know what time it is?*
               B: *No, what time is it?*
               A: *No, I was asking* **you.**

(155)   A: *Do you know what today is?*
               B: *Yeah, the start of National Pickle Week.*
               A: *Aw, I was going to surprise you.*

An example of another peculiar pseudo-question found in some dialects is B's reply in the following dialogue:

(156)   A: *Did Martha call today?*
                         B: *Is the Pope Catholic?*

B's utterance has a double value. First, it is an affirmative answer, and second, it indicates that that answer was obvious. This additional sense is clear from that fact that such a response is odd in dialogue (157).

(157)   A: *Is the hull speed of a boat proportional to the square root of its length on the waterline?*
        B: *?Is the Pope Catholic?*

There is some room for originality in the construction of these interrogative answers, but additional material characteristic of serious questions is disallowed. None of the following would have worked in dialogue (156):

(158)   *Is the Pope Catholic, or not?*
(159)   *Is the Pope Catholic, by any chance?*
(160)   *Could you tell me if the Pope is Catholic?*

In this case, however, I would hesitate to say that B's response in (157) is the **semantic** equivalent of an affirmative answer. This is because there is a fairly natural conversational explanation for the effect of such sentences. B's response is clearly a *non sequitur*, and therefore, A is forced to think of how to make sense of the utterance in context. Just about the only way of making conversational sense of a *non sequitur* as a response to a question is to assume that it is a hint. This holds, not only for interrogatives, but for declaratives that do not seem responsive as well. Thus, if a child asks how much nine times nine is, a not infelicitous response might be the *non sequitur*, *nine times* ten *is ninety*. What might have started out as a fairly normal conversation has then become a sort of Socratic guessing game, the object of which is to lead the original questioner to the right answer. B's response in (156) has the same effect. But the quiz in this case is very easy, and the hint a dead giveaway—hence the connotation that the answer to the original question was obvious. Notice that if B's response is a **quiz** question, then the fact that (158), (159), and (160) are not equivalent to B's response in (156) is explained.

IMPERATIVE SENTENCES

Sentences that lack an overt subject, but whose logical subject refers to the addressee, and that contain a verb form homophonous with the infinitive are traditionally called "imperatives." But there seem to be many linguistically and pragmatically distinct speech acts that this sentence type encodes. The communicative function of instructional sentences, such as those one finds in recipes and manuals and on labels, stands, for example, in sharp contrast to the function of requests. Instructions of the kind in question are issued for the addressee's benefit, and not for the speaker's. Instructions are understood to be applicable whenever the addressee undertakes a certain kind of project, whereas ordinary requests are one-shot affairs (unless there is some explicit mention that they are to be taken as standing, contingent orders). A series of instructions is ordinarily understood as a sequence of steps to be carried out in order, whereas, unless some specific sequence is explicitly mentioned, multiple requests are not taken as applying serially.

Alongside of these functional distinctions, we find exactly the sorts of formal distinctions between instructions and requests that were described in Chapter 5 as reflective of differing semantics. There are, for one thing, several transformational rules that are sensitive to whether an imperative-form sentence is intended as a request or as an instruction. Some of these rules are needed in the grammar of English anyway and thus provide especially cogent arguments for an underlying semantic difference of the right kind. Imperatives with a request sense idiosyncratically fail to allow adverb preposing, while this rule applies regularly in the case of imperatives with an instructional sense. Example (163) is ambiguous in this regard, but (164) has only an instructional reading:

(163)   *Remove the lid carefully.*
(164)   *Carefully remove the lid.*

A second phenomenon, perhaps partially related to the first, reduces the first of two conjoined sentences that express simultaneous or consecutive actions performed by the same agent(s) to a participial verb phrase. It seems clear that a series of rules is involved here, with equi-NP deletion operating as part of the reduction. The whole set of processes is required to account for the relationship obtaining between the following sentences:

(165)   *Angus shouldered his pipes and adjusted his filibeg.*
(166)   *Shouldering his pipes, Angus adjusted his filibeg.*

Now, observe that this process (or set of processes) does not affect imperative-form sentences that are understood as requests: (167) is ambiguous, but (168) has only an instructional sense.

(167)   *Hold the deck in the left hand and deal three cards to each player.*

(168) *Holding the deck in the left hand, deal three cards to each player.*

There are also some unique deletion rules that affect instructional sentences on labels and in directions such as recipes. In the latter case, the patient noun phrase of an instructional sentence may be deleted if it is coreferent with the patient noun phrase of an immediately preceding instruction. Two examples of this are

(169) *Separate the whites of three eggs. Beat until foamy.*
(170) *Turn the gear until the mark points down and remove with tool No. 527.*

On labels, a very similar process deletes patient noun phrases that refer to the item to which the label is affixed, or to the contents of the container to which the label is affixed.[7] Examples (171) and (172) are two standard instructions to which the deletion rule has applied.

(171)   *Keep out of the reach of children.*
(172)   *Shake well before using.*

The cooccurrence properties of requests are, as we might expect, not shared by instructional sentences bearing any of the grammatical earmarks of instructions. Similarly, grammatical phenomena characteristic of requests and grammatical phenomena characteristic of instructions cannot be found in the same sentence. All of the following are less than fully grammatical.

(173)   *?Please do not use near fire or flame.*
(174)   *?*Stirring constantly, please bring to a boil.*
(175)   *?Use sparingly, would you?*
(176)   *?Take before meals, someone.*

---

[7] Note the truly unusual condition on this rule: It involves not only grammatical constructs, but real-world objects as well.

There is another deletion rule operative on labels that seems to be distinct from the patient-deletion rule that I am discussing here. This rule deletes subjects of declarative-form sentences that provide some important information. Note that it is the surface subject position that defines the domain of this rule:

(a)   *Bottled in Peoria by H. and P. Distillers.*
(b)   *°H. and P. Distillers bottled in Peoria.*

The subject-deletion rule would seem to be allowed in any telegraphic style. It operates, for example, in headlines such as the following:

(c)   *Eats baby's food, father of eleven confesses.*

The label and recipe rules, however, are restricted to sentences with a certain illocutionary force.

Instructions, therefore, constitute a separate sentence type in English, albeit a very subtly distinguished one.

I have not been able to decide whether the instructions on labels form a class apart from the instructions in manuals, recipes, and so on. They are certainly very similar in grammatical behavior. The two deletion rules, for example, are identically constrained. Neither can produce a violation of the coordinate structure constraint (see Ross, 1968).

(177)   *Keep and other medications out of the reach of children.

(178)   *Thicken sauce with arrowroot and return and spices to pan.

Neither can delete the object of a preposition:

(179)   *Take water with.
(180)   *Shuffle the deck and put the extra card near.

Both rules can delete the subject of an adverbial clause if the main verb in the clause is the copula. If the subject is deleted, the copula must be deleted too. The following sentence would be appropriate either on a label or in a set of instructions:

(181)   Shake until thoroughly mixed.

The similarity of the restrictions on the two deletion rules is not very convincing evidence that they are the same rule, though. Most of these restrictions correspond to general grammatical strategies of English. If, for example, we were to catalogue the cases in which there are relative clauses without a relative marker, we would find a very similar set of restrictions. Thus, when the relative clause is the surface object of a preposition, it may not be deleted:

(182)   *The girl with I saw Bill. . . .
(183)   The girl with whom I saw Bill. . . .

And if the relative item is the subject of the verb be, it may be deleted only if the verb is deleted as well.

(184)   *The dog is sitting on the rug is a Samoyed.
(185)   The dog sitting on the rug is a Samoyed.

I wish to consider next the problem of determining the range of encoded speech-act values of sentences like the following:

(186)   Feed my dog and I'll show you my home movies.
(187)   If you feed my dog I'll show you my home movies.

The following terms have been used to describe formally similar sentences: pseudo-imperative, threat, warning, and promise. Indeed, it is possible to invent situations under which one or another of these terms most appropriately describes the linguistic performance. For example, if A does not want B to feed his (A's) dog, and if A knows B to have a decided dislike for his (A's) home movies, then it would seem correct to call A's utterance of either sentence to B a threat. Now, suppose that A does not personally care whether B feeds A's dog, but knows that B really hates A's home movies. Suppose, further, that A is under the influence of a posthypnotic suggestion that he is aware of. Whenever anyone feeds A's dog, A involuntarily shows Fido's benefactor his home movies. Now we might be inclined to say that A's saying (186) or (187) to B constitutes a warning. This situation is admittedly pretty farfetched. Perhaps the threat–warning distinction is a bit more realistic for the following sentence:

(188) *Hit me in the knee with that little hammer and I'll kick you in the chin.*

If the speaker of (188) is talking about a particularly strong reflex of his, the sentence is a warning. If he is talking about something malicious that he intends to do, the sentence is a threat.

Returning now to (186) and (187), if A wants his dog fed, and thinks that B would like to see his films, A's utterance of either sentence to B might be called a promise (better: a contingent promise or contingent offer). Though it exists, the pseudo-imperative or conditional reading for (186) and (187) also demands a rather absurd context, so will again refer to a different sentence that brings out the interpretation more clearly.

(189)   *Do your homework and you'll get a good grade.*

This sentence could be a student's theory about the way a certain course is graded. The sentence need not be spoken to a student enrolled in that course at all. Here, the sentence has a true implicational reading, paraphrasable as *Anyone who does his homework gets a good grade.* But the sentence could also be a promise, as when it is uttered by a teacher to a student.

Which of these descriptions of acts performed by uttering (186) or (187) corresponds to a separate illocutionary force of these sentences? For which of these, in other words, are we to posit separate abstract performative verbs?

If we employ the formal criteria of Chapter 5 in identifying syntactic meaning, then it would appear to be the case that there are three separate illocutionary forces involved: the pseudo-imperative or true implicational reading, the contingent-promise reading, and one that covers both the threat and warning cases.

G. Lakoff (1966) has argued (apparently) that sentences of the form (186) with stative verbs are not true imperatives, on the basis of the fact that they do not occur with such typically imperative features as the tag *will you?*

(190)   *Be tall, won't you (?), and you'll make the basketball team.*

But with nonstative verbs in the first conjunct, imperative characteristics are found:[8]

(191)   *(Please) Do your homework, won't you, and you'll get a good grade.*

As we might expect, this sentence is now unambiguous, having only the contingent-promise sense. Therefore, whimperative formation and fracturing must be sensitive to the distinction between the conditional use and the contingent-promise use of a sentence like (191)—that is, this aspect of significance must be part of the meaning of the sentence under the form-follows-function doctrine.

The positive and negative uses of sentences like (187) are also sharply distinguished. As R. Lakoff (1969b) has shown only the negative use, the threat or warning interpretations, allow apparently spurious negative-polarity items in the antecedent. This holds not only for *any*, the item she discussed, but also for strong negative-polarity items. The following sentence can be understood only as a threat or a warning.

(192)   *If you move a muscle I'll shoot.*

And it holds for coordinate forms like (186), as well as for conditionals. Example (193) is also unambiguously an attempt to deter the addressee from moving.

(193)   *Move a muscle and I'll shoot.*

A final peculiarity of warnings is that in negative first disjuncts, the second-person subject may appear after the fronted auxiliary:

---

[8] The imperative reading of sentences like (182) is not discussed in G. Lakoff (1966). Consequently, it is difficult to tell whether that author would have regarded these sentences as ambiguous—as I am doing—or not.

(194)   *Don't you tease my dog* $\begin{cases} \text{\textit{or I'll tell my mommy.}} \\ \text{?? \textit{and I'll give you a}} \\ \text{\textit{lollipop.}} \end{cases}$

The second disjunct—that is, the part that corresponds to the consequent in the conditional form—need not appear. Thus, the following string is grammatical, and unambiguously a threat or warning.

(195)   *Don't you tease my dog.*

I have claimed that, while the threat–warning use of sentences like (186) is a distinct illocutionary type,[9] threats are not distinct from warnings as far as sentence meaning is concerned. It is much more difficult to argue that this is so, since my claim is based on the lack of any grammatical phenomena that distinguish these two significances. What this means is simply that I am not **aware** of any such phenomena. If some come to light, I will, of course, have to recant on this point.

But what is the difference between a threat and a warning if they are not separate illocutionary acts? It seems to me that it is this: We describe as threats warnings for which we assume that the warner has control over the consequences of not heeding the warning. In a similar way, we may describe acts of asserting as blurtings out just in case the assertion was made hastily and, to some extent, against the blurter's desires. Yet clearly, there is no illocutionary act of blurting out. I am claiming, then, that it is not a random fact that English lacks a surface performative verb *threaten*, but rather that this is reflective of the fact that there is no abstract performative verb with the appropriate sense. I am also claiming that it is not accidental that we can use the surface performative verb *warn* to threaten, as in (196).

(196) *I warn you that if you don't marry my daughter I'll shoot.*

[9] A separate semantic structure for implicit warnings that come out looking like conditionals is provided in R. Lakoff (1969b), as well. Lakoff points, aptly, to the similar behavior of such sentences to the complements of the surface verb *warn*. But she also uses the word *threat* in regard to these sentences, so I do not know whether she intended there to be an abstract relative of the verb *threaten*, too, or whether, as seems more likely, she would have agreed with me in claiming that the same meaning is involved in performances that we describe as threats as in those that we describe as warnings.

Finally, I wish to point out that military orders constitute a separate speech-act type, distinguished syntactically by the fact they allow the fronting of certain adverbials that cannot otherwise be fronted.

(197)   *Right face.*
(198)   **Right Bill faced.*

Such orders do not occur in whimperative form, nor do they cooccur with *please*.

7

Conclusions

Despite the inconclusiveness of a great deal of the foregoing, the linguistic theory of speech acts has a lot to say about the use of language. It is my purpose here to reiterate and refine the principal claims about natural-language pragmatics that this theory makes.

First of all, the theory propounded here asserts that illocutionary force is an aspect of meaning, represented, like all other aspects of meaning, as part of the most remote syntactic structure. The illocutionary force of an uttered sentence is not distinct from propositional acts, to use Searle's (1970) term, nor from one sort of locutionary act, to use Austin's (1965) term. In pronouncing a sentence with a particular illocutionary force, a speaker refers to himself and his addressee, and predicates the illocutionary act of these two and a sentential argument. In the majority of cases, however, the acts of reference and predication are abstract, in the sense that the corresponding referring expressions and predicating expressions fail to show up in the surface form of the sentence. The illocutionary force of a sentence, in all cases, has reflexes in surface structure, although these reflexes may be quite subtle and often ambiguous. The relationship between meaning and form is as intricate and indirect in this case as

147

it has been found to be in the case of nonpragmatic aspects of meaning.

The portion of the underlying syntacto-semantic tree that represents the illocutionary force of a sentence is recognizable by its topological properties. The main predicate involved in establishing the force of the sentence is the highest agentive predicate in the semantic representation — that is, the unique predicate that is in a clause that is the object of abstract DO, which itself is not dominated by another clause containing abstract DO.

In the previous chapter, I showed that two of the major surface-syntactic sentence types actually encode a rather large number of distinct illocutionary forces. (I am convinced that the declarative sentence type represents a wide range of forces as well, but I have not as yet conducted a detailed investigation of their syntactic correlates.) We saw that orders, requests, instructions, warnings, and contingent promises were all distinct illocutionary types in English. In a way, this is a counterintuitive result, since there is a unifying pragmatic aspect to all of these speech acts, and it is consequently no surprise that they all appear in the same syntactic clothing, even if the accessories are different. An opponent of the system of analysis to which I am committed might well charge that the inescapable conclusion that these various uses of imperative sentences correspond to separate illocutionary forces amounts to a *reductio ad absurdum*.

A second disturbing property of these analyses concerns the fact that the formal properties that distinguish the various subtypes of illocutionary acts are not mutually exclusive. Most of the syntactic properties involved are neither necessary nor sufficient for adjudging a sentence to be of a particular type. What we find, instead, are partially overlapping properties that can be displayed on a graph such as (1), where each line is what I shall call an **isogen**, a line that encloses a set of speech-act types that share a syntactic property.

The diagram indicates, for example, that requests and suggestions are alike in that they can appear in superficial interrogative form (e.g., *Would you S? or Why don't you* S?), that warnings and contingent promises are alike in their ability to surface in conditional form (e.g., *If you give me a drink I'll show you my slides of Colorado*), and so on. Of course, this map is not complete. Isogen 10, for example, should enclose additional speech-act types that can appear as interrogative sentences — for example, true questions and requestions. In fact, a complete isogenic map would include all illocutionary types.

Now, by merely postulating separate abstract performative predi-

(1)

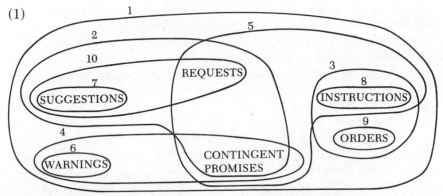

1 = imperative form
2 = fractured whimperative form
3 = adverb fronting
4 = conditional form
5 = sentence-adverbial *please*

6 = disjunctive form
7 = inclusive first-person subjects
8 = object deletion
9 = special adverb fronting
10 = interrogative form

cates, such as SUGGEST, WARN, REQUEST, ORDER, and so forth, the pragmatic similarity that, in some cases, is obviously involved in the syntactic resemblances diagramed in (1) is obscured. Looked at from a still less favorable light, the setting up of distinct abstract performatives makes the dubious claim that the distribution of the formal features that demarcate each class is entirely accidental. It provides no account whatever of why, for example, contingent promises behave like warnings with respect to some syntactic properties, and like suggestions and requests with respect to others.

Fortunately, there is a straightforward way of circumventing these difficulties. Generative semantics allows one to claim that lexical items—most especially verbs—are semantically complex, and there is nothing, as far as I can see, that would prevent one from claiming that **abstract** predicates are complex as well. Then, in the case of the majority of abstract predicates that can manifest themselves by allowing their underlying complements to appear in imperative form, a more basic predicate could be set up as a component. The aspects of force that all imperative sentences share, and the imperative form itself, could then be traced to this more basic predicate. By way of illustration, I will consider one example where I believe the semantic decomposability of an abstract performative verb is motivated.

Impressionistically speaking, what all of the senses of imperative-form sentences that appear in (1) have in common is that they indicate that the speaker is prescribing with his sentence some future course of action for the addressee. Let me use the now-traditional label IMPERE for an abstract predicate that expresses just this much. But these illocutionary acts differ in the (covertly) communicated reason for the prescription. Requests, for instance, are understood as prescriptions that would benefit the speaker if carried out, while suggestions are understood as being made at least partially for the addressee's benefit.

Consider now what warnings are. They are not merely acts of apprising an addressee of a dangerous situation, but are always understood as advising appropriate action, such as, minimally, being on one's guard. Note the difference between informing someone of a volcanic eruption and warning him of it. The surface verb *warn*, in fact, can take complements that express the suggested action, as in (2) and (3).

(2)   *I warn you not to touch my daughter.*
(3)   *I warn you that you should be on the lookout for hapo-lopses.*

It should be observed that this range of complements — an infinitival complement with obligatory Equi-NP deletion using a higher indirect object as antecedent, and a *that* complement containing the modal *should* — is exactly the range of complements that the verb *say* takes when it is used to report imperative speech acts:

(4)   *Mommy says to stop eating mud.*
(5)   *The chancellor said that we should admit anyone who could pay tuition.*

The notification of a dangerous or potentially unpleasant state of affairs, which is also involved in the meaning of a warning, is one aspect of the ostensible reason for the speaker's impering. A warning conveys the idea that not behaving appropriately would bring about results, stemming from the dangerous situation, that the addressee is assumed not to desire. Again, the range of complements that surface *warn* can take reflects exactly this.

(6)   *I warn you not to ask me any more questions or I'll make/*let you study linguistics.*
(7)   *I warn you that if you eat pork you'll ?enjoy yourself/suffer the rest of your life.*

Nonexplicit warnings behave identically. Example (8) is ungrammatical with *let*, but grammatical with *make*.

(8) *Don't ask me any more questions or I'll make/*let you
study linguistics.*

And (9) can be understood as a warning only if the addressee is assumed to be some sort of masochist.

(9) *If you eat pork you'll enjoy yourself the rest of your life.*

The lexical verb *warn* can take both a complement clause reflective of an imperative structure and a reason-for-speech-act adverbial of conditional form. The antecedent in this conditional can be the negative of the complement clause, but cannot be the same as the complement clause:

(10) *I warn you not to touch my daughter because if you
do/*don't I'll take you to Brooklyn.*

Taking all of these facts into consideration, I propose that warnings, whether realized with the lexical item *warn* or not, are to be semantically represented as acts of impering, which act the speaker justifies by indicating that failure to follow the prescription would have certain consequences. The speaker's assumption that these consequences are objectionable to the addressee need not be stated directly in the semantic structure, since if the speaker did not hold this belief, he would have to hold two contradictory beliefs. The proposed semantic structure of warnings (passing over numerous difficulties involving causation, tense, and so on) is represented in (11).

(11)

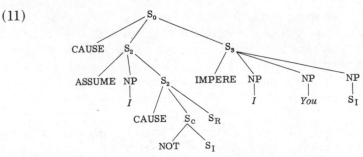

I propose, further, that the sole difference between warnings and what I have called "contingent promises" is that the latter lack the abstract negative predicate in the first argument of S_2. Again, the speaker's assumption about the desirability of the result S_R would be superfluous. Notice that the obligatory presence of a negative in warnings, and its obligatory absence in corresponding promises, can help to explain the fact, observed some time ago by R. Lakoff (1969b), that the negative-polarity items force a warning interpretation in sentences like (12).

(12)   *Take some/any cookies and I'll whip you.*

If analyses like this prove correct, we must conclude that the precise speech-act type of a sentence involves not only the identity of the highest agentive predicate, but the identity of any higher adverbial modifiers as well. In general, then, the range of illocutionary force in a language is not matched by a similar range of atomic performative predicates.

This discussion has concerned itself entirely with illocutionary force — the pragmatic meaning of sentences. But what is an illocutionary **act**, in terms of linguistic theory? Certainly, it is not simply the propositional acts involved in the illocutionary force of an uttered sentence, for such acts would be automatically successful upon completion of the utterance. Illocutionary acts are supposed to be capable of failing to be felicitous, to secure uptake, to take effect. In this respect, they are similar to perlocutionary effects. There is another way in which illocutionary acts resemble perlocutionary acts: The effect of both is posterior to the speech act. In most cases, the perlocutionary effects and the secural of uptake of the illocutionary act are **immediately** posterior to the act of speech, and give the impression of simultaneity with it, but there are cases where there is a noticeable lag. The perlocutionary effect of amusing someone by telling a joke is one case in point. Among illocutionary acts, the same delay can be observed in the performance of the illocutionary act of christening a ship. Under one set of conventions, this effect is not achieved until the bottle breaks on the stem of the ship. If it fails to, the act of uttering *I christen thee . . .* does not achieve the christening and must be repeated. The illocutionary act in such cases is just as much the by-product of the utterance as are any perlocutionary effects.

Austin wished to distinguish between illocutionary and perlocutionary acts on the basis of whether one describes the act as having been accomplished **in** saying something (illocutionary acts) or **by** saying something (perlocutionary acts). While it does seem strange to describe clearly perlocutionary effects as having been done in saying something, the following sorts of sentences strike me as perfectly normal:

(13)   *By saying, "I now pronounce you man and wife" Reverend Kornblatt pronounced them man and wife.*

(14) *By saying, "The evening star is bald," Fred asserted*
      that the evening star was bald.

Illocutionary acts, then, have all the characteristics of perlocutionary
acts, but not vice versa. I suggest, then, that an illocutionary act is a
special kind of perlocutionary act, with characteristics that distinguish it from all other kinds of perlocutions, just as illocutionary
force is a circumscribable kind of meaning.

Some perlocutionary effects can be brought off independently of,
or even in spite of, the meaning of an utterance, as when one yells in
the ear of a sleeping person, *Don't wake up.* One can succeed in
frightening someone by saying *Boo!,* but it is clearly not the meaning
of the utterance (if it is even proper to speak of its having a meaning)
that is responsible for the success of the perlocution. On the other
hand, there are perlocutionary effects whose success depends crucially on the meaning of an utterance. Many—but not all—kinds of
jokes succeed in amusing because of what they mean. Or, to take a
different sort of example, if I am known to be an inveterate liar, I
could convince my audience that it was raining by saying *It isn't
raining,* yet a sentence with a different meaning—say, *The cat is on
the mat*—would fail utterly to accomplish this. I will call perlocutionary effects whose success depends on the meaning of an utterance **sense perlocutions.** Under the view that illocutionary force is an
aspect of sentence meaning, illocutionary acts are sense perlocutions.

An especially important proper subset of the set of sense perlocutions consists of effects whose success involves the aspect of
meaning called "force." Illocutionary acts are quite obviously
members of this set; that is, they are **force perlocutions.** To see that
there are sense perlocutions that are not force perlocutions, consider
the usefulness of presupposed semantic material. If there is no
reason to doubt a speaker's presuppositions, we usually simply assume that they are correct. That is, we become convinced of their
correctness. But what is presupposed material is, by definition, independent of the illocutionary force of the sentence in which it is
found. All of the following sentences communicate a presupposition
on the part of the speaker that Morton owns a Picasso. For this
reason, they may all equally well be used to get the addressee to
believe that Morton owns a Picasso.

(15)   *Sam saw Morton's Picasso.*
(16)   *Did you see Morton's Picasso?*
(17)   *Take a look at Morton's Picasso.*
(18)   *I promise to look at Morton's Picasso.*

Now, while every illocutionary act is a force perlocution, not every force perlocution is an illocutionary act. The most typical examples of perlocutionary acts in the old, narrower sense that excludes illocutionary acts turn out to be force perlocutions, in fact. A certain question (e.g., *Are you old enough to drink?*) might be insulting to a 21-year-old, while the corresponding assertion would not be. Similarly, a certain promise might please an addressee by virtue of its being a promise, where another illocutionary act would fail to have this effect just because it is not a promise. What distinguishes illocutionary acts from other sorts of force perlocutions is, first, the automaticity of the success of the act and, second, the very direct relationship between the act performed and the illocutionary force of the uttered sentence. For an illocutionary act to succeed, all that is required is the uttering of a sentence with a certain force under certain conventional conditions. These conditions (the felicity conditions) are established by society, are finite in number, and are generally such that it can be determined beforehand whether they are satisfied or not. It is for this reason that speakers are always held responsible for their illocutionary acts. While there are conditions on the successful performance of nonillocutionary perlocutionary acts, such as, say, that an addressee be sensitive about something in order to be offended by its mention, these conditions are neither conventional nor, in general, such that it can be infallibly determined beforehand that they have been met. The relationship between the illocutionary force of an utterance and the illocutionary act that is thereby performed is direct, in the sense that having predicated the performance of the act of himself, the speaker has performed an act describable by the same predicate. Subsequent to the utterance of a sentence with the illocutionary force f, if the felicity conditions have been met, then it is correct to say that the utterer has f'ed.

The illocutionary force of a sentence has the unique ability to change the real world. In general, the relationship between the meanings of uttered sentences and the real world is much more tenuous. For the most part, the meaning of an utterance is at double remove from facts about the real world. By uttering sentences with particular meanings, speakers convey aspects of their beliefs and attitudes. But this, of course, is a far cry from their actually having those attitudes or holding those beliefs. It is a serious mistake to claim that attitudes, beliefs, and so on find direct reflection in linguistic form. Rather, it is what we wish to do with our utterances that determines which, if any, or our feelings and estimations of the world we express through the medium of language. And because a speaker's true

beliefs and attitudes are by no means indicative of real states of affairs, it is an even more serious error to pretend that **situations** have a
direct influence on the forms of language. While locutions like *If a
speaker believes that there are unicorns, he says* Y or *If it has just
stopped raining, the speaker would say* Z might be convenient, they
and their kin should be prevented from masquerading as truthful
representations of the way language functions.

The direct relationship between an illocutionary act and the illocutionary force of an uttered sentence partially vindicates Austin's
much-discussed claim that illocutionary acts are conventional acts
(see, for example, Strawson, 1964). According to the point of view of
the present work, illocutionary acts are conventional not only in that
the conditions that guarantee their success are conventional, but also
in that they are directly related to aspects of meaning that, by the
definition I have been using, always manifest themselves in terms of
formal properties of sentences — that is, according to the conventions
of a language.

Austin's famous attempt at stating the nature of the conventionality
of illocutionary acts is seen to be false in the light of the linguistic
theory I have propounded. To quote Austin (1965:103), an illocutionary act ". . . can be said to be *conventional*, in the sense that at
least it could be made explicit by the performative formula; . . ."
But we have seen that there are many cases where a specific illocutionary force with grammatical consequences is not matched by a
grammatical explicit performative. Requestions and instructions are
two illocutionary-force types that are not matched by any lexical performative verb. There are also near-performatives, sentences that just
miss being pronounceable in the performative formula owing to the
vagaries of a particular language. The sentence

(19)   *You're fired.*

should certainly be assigned the semantic structure in which the
illocutionary-force-defining verb is *fire* (or its semantically complex
source), yet, idiosyncratically, we cannot say

(20)   **I fire you.*

Now, it would not help to claim that (19) is an explicit performative,
because that notion is weak enough as it is. From the standpoint of
the linguistic theory of speech acts, the source of the weakness of the
notions **explicit performative** and (surface) **performative verb** is quite
obvious; these are semantic concepts, and any definition of them
directly in terms of surface syntax would necessarily have to incor-

porate a great deal of the grammar—the system relating meaning and form. It is, therefore, no more reasonable to expect to be able to define the notion of a performative directly in terms of surface syntax than to do the same for the semantic notion **quantifier.**

There is a great deal left to be done in the investigation of the theory of abstract performative clauses. Not only are there lines of research here that I have followed only for a short distance, but there are whole directions that I have not taken. I have only scratched the surface of the problem of determining the range of abstract illocutionary acts in English, and I have done nothing at all to determine how this range matches the range in other languages. It is conceivable that all languages share the same abstract illocutionary structures, but the results obtained in Chapter 6 make that hypothesis look quite problematic. I would guess, for example, that the interrogative-form sentences that I called "requestions" are a rather recent acquisition in English. After all, it is hard to imagine why there would have been a need for such a specialized illocutionary act until the advent of mass education and the proliferation of surveys, quiz shows, and the like.

Notice, though, that the range of basic illocutionary-act-defining predicates that were partially involved in the sentences of imperative form that were investigated in Chapter 6 is much smaller. I have the feeling that a comprehensive account of the decomposability of abstract performatives would present a similar picture. While the range of non-explicitly represented illocutionary forces might seem surprisingly large, the number of atomic agentive predicates involved might be gratifyingly small. Whether these more basic performatives are universal in range is a separate question—and one that I think is more likely to receive an affirmative answer.

The semantic decomposability of abstract performatives also holds out the hope of allowing a natural classification of illocutionary acts. A classification based on semantic commonality, as reflected in syntactic commonality, would make considerably more sense than the sort of impressionistic classifications (such as the one in Austin, 1965) that have heretofore been given.

This entire study has been predicated on some important assumptions about meaning—namely, that sentences **have** meaning and that it is the job of the linguist to elucidate the relationship between the sentence and its meaning. Part of what was required in order to study the aspects of meaning that we call "force" was some means of distinguishing between meaning and other types of significance associated with sentences. An important spinoff of this study, I feel, is the set of criteria that were developed in Chapter 5 as guidelines for determining which part of the significance of sentences is to be called meaning. These criteria are roughly those that have been invoked by linguists in the past 15 years, so I see the present work as fundamentally conservative. It may, of course, turn out that these criteria do not lead to an enlightening level of semantic representation. It may even turn out that some of our most cherished notions about the relationship between meaning and form will fall. One apparent tenet of modern formal linguistics, for example, has been that a particular sentence uttered on a particular occasion has but one meaning. Recently, however, just this tenet has been called into question by a researcher in linguistic pragmatics. Weiser (1973) has examined sentences like the following, which she calls double assertions:

(21) *Bill just told me that there was a fight here last night.*

She argues persuasively that this sentence is ambiguous as to what is being asserted or announced; either the speaker is informing his audience both that there was a fight and that the speaker has just learned about it from Bill, or he is informing his addressee only that Bill made an announcement of some fact, which perhaps was well known to both speaker and addressee. Now, the utility of such sentences as (21), Weiser points out, lies in their being ambiguous and allowing one to avoid neatly an illocutionary faux pas. It is ordinarily irritating for an addressee to be told something he is already well aware of, just as it is irritating to be asked to do something that one is in the process of doing, or to be asked a question to which one has just given the answer. Now, if the speaker is not sure whether his addressee knows that there was a fight, and wants to tell him that there was without risking offending him, he could use a sentence like (21). If the addressee was not previously aware of the fight, he would become aware of it by hearing (21). If he knew about it already, though, (21) could be taken simply as an assertion that Bill made some announcement, and since this is new information, the addressee could not take offense.

.As far as linguistic theory is concerned, the problem is how to indicate that the importance of a sentence involves two semantic structures and not one. This is the same problem that must be faced in dealing eventually with puns, double-entendres, codes, and purposeful ambiguity in poetry. Are these facts merely a matter of language use, or does part of a speaker's knowledge of the language include rules for systematically exploiting certain ambiguities?

The answer to this question has a direct bearing on the treatment of speech-act idioms, such as whimperatives and queclaratives. I have represented speech-act idioms as strictly analogous to other sorts of idioms. Idioms arise from metaphors through a process of resemanticization. Given the one-sentence–one-meaning postulate of generative semantics, it is necessary to assume that this resemanticization takes place in one quantum jump; a metaphor suddenly loses its original sense and simultaneously gains the new, idiomatic sense. If our theory were allowed to claim that a single sense of a sentence resided in more than one semantic representation, a somewhat more realistic account of the progress of a construction from metaphor to idiom could be given. Such a mode would allow us to claim that as the original meaning gradually grows weaker, the new meaning correspondingly gains strength. The number of formal properties that correlate with the apparent sense compared to the number that depend on the idiomatic sense would be a measure of the relative strengths of the two underlying semantic representations. Whimperatives, for example, behave almost entirely like the requests for which they are used, but also display a few of the formal properties of the questions that they appear to be. This might be taken as an indication that the request sense of such sentences has grown very strong, but that a trace of the historically prior question sense remains.

Such a theory would stand to the theory presented in this work as a general theory to a special theory. As such, it would necessarily incorporate the present theory's claims about the relationship between the aspect of meaning that we call "force" and the syntax of natural languages. In particular, it would have to amplify on the claim, made repeatedly here, that a great deal of specific information about what we are doing with the sentences we use is encoded in, and conveyed by, those sentences. The complexity of our interactions involving speech is reflected in the complexity of the grammar of speech acts.

References

Austin, J. L. *How to do things with words,* J. O. Urmson (Ed.). New York: Oxford, 1965.

Baker, C. L. Double negatives. *Linguistic Inquiry,* 1970, I, 169–187.

Baker, C. L., and Brame, Michael K. "Global rules": A rejoinder. *Language,* 1972, **48,** 51–76.

Barthelme, Donald. *Snow White.* New York: Atheneum, 1967.

Binnick, Robert I., Davison, Alice, Green, Georgia M., and Morgan, Jerry L. (Eds.). *Papers from the fifth regional meeting of the Chicago Linguistic Society.* Chicago: Univ. of Chicago Department of Linguistics, 1969.

Bolinger, Dwight. The imperative in English. In *To honor Roman Jakobson.* The Hague: Mouton, 1967. Pp. 335–362.

Bresnan, Joan W. Sentence stress and syntactic transformations. *Language,* 1971, **47,** 257–282.

Burt, Marina K. *From deep to surface structure: An introduction to transformational syntax.* New York: Harper & Row, 1971.

Carroll, Lewis. *The annotated Alice: Alice's adventures in Wonderland and Through the looking glass, with an introduction and notes by Martin Gardner.* New York: Clarkson N. Potter, 1960.

Chomsky, Noam. *Syntactic structures.* (Janua linguarum 4.) The Hague: Mouton, 1957.

Cohen, David. The mis-representation of presuppositions as a projection problem. Unpublished Xerox. Univ. of Wisconsin (Milwaukee), 1972.

159

Cohen, L. Jonathan. Do illocutionary forces exist? In Jay F. Rosenberg and Charles Travis (Eds.), *Readings in the philosophy of language*. Englewood Cliffs, N.J.: Prentice-Hall, 1971. Pp. 580–599.

Cohen, Ted. Illocutions and perlocutions. *Foundations of Language*, 1973, **9**, 492–503.

Costa, Rachel M. Let's solve let's. *Papers in Linguistics*, 1972, **5**, 141–145.

Davison, Alice. Performative verbs, adverbs and felicity conditions: An inquiry into the nature of performative verbs. Unpublished Ph.D. dissertation. University of Chicago, 1972.

Donnellan, Keith S. Reference and definite descriptions. In Jay F. Rosenberg and Charles Travis (Eds.), *Readings in the philosophy of language*. Englewood Cliffs, N.J.: Prentice-Hall, 1971. Pp. 195–212.

Elliott, Dale Eugene. The grammar of emotive and exclamatory sentences in English. *Working Papers in Linguistics*, 1971, 8, vii–111. Columbus: The Ohio State University Computer and Information Science Research Center.

Fillmore, Charles J. The position of embedding transformations in a grammar. *Word*, 1963, **19**, 208–232.

Fraser, Bruce. *An examination of the performative analysis*. Bloomington, Ind.: Indiana University Linguistics Club, 1971.

Fraser, Bruce. Idioms within a transformational grammar. *Foundations of language*, 1970, **6**, 22–43.

Gallagher, Mary. Does meaning grow on trees? In Jerrold M. Sadock and Anthony L. Vanek (Eds.), *Studies presented to Robert B. Lees by his Students*. Edmonton, Canada: Linguistic Research, 1970. Pp. 79–95.

Geis, Michael Lorenz. Adverbial subordinate clauses in English. Unpublished Ph.D. dissertation. Massachusetts Institute of Technology, 1970.

Gordon, David, and Lakoff, George. Conversational postulates. In *Papers from the seventh regional meeting of the Chicago Linguistic Society*. Chicago: Chicago Linguistic Society, 1971. Pp. 63–85.

Green, Georgia M. How to get people to do things with words. In Roger W. Shuy (Ed.), *New directions in linguistics*. Washington: Georgetown Univ. Press, 1973. Pp. 51–81.

Grice, H. P. Logic and conversation. Unpublished manuscript. 1968.

Harada, S. I. Where do vocatives come from? *English Linguistics* (Tokyo), 1971, **5**, 2–44.

Hasegawa, Kinsuke. Transformations and semantic interpretation. *Linguistic Inquiry*, 1972, **III**, 141–161.

Heringer, James T. Some grammatical correlates of felicity conditions and presuppositions. *Working Papers in Linguistics*, 1972, **II**, iv–111. Columbus: The Ohio State University Department of Linguistics.

Horn, Laurence R. On the semantic properties of logical operators in English. Unpublished Ph.D. dissertation. Univ. of California (Los Angeles), 1972.

Jacobs, Roderick A., and Rosenbaum, Peter S. *Readings in English transformational grammar*. Waltham, Mass.: Ginn, 1970.

Jakobson, Roman. Shifters, verbal categories, and the Russian verb. In Roman Jakobson, *Selected writings. Vol. II. Word and language*. The Hague: Mouton, 1971. Pp. 130–148.

Jespersen, Otto. *The philosophy of grammar*. London: George Allen & Unwin, 1963.

Karttunen, Lauri. Implicative verbs. *Language,* 1971, **47**, 340–359.

Karttunen, Lauri. Presuppositions of compound sentences. *Linguistic Inquiry,* 1973, **IV**, 169–195.

Katz, Jerrold J., and Postal, Paul M. *An integrated theory of linguistic descriptions.* Research monograph no. 26. Cambridge: M.I.T. Press, 1964.

Kimball, John P. Categories of meaning. Unpublished Ph.D. dissertation. Massachusetts Institute of Technology, 1970.

Kiparsky, Paul, and Kiparsky, Carol. Fact. In Manfred Bierwisch and Karl Erich Heidolph, (Eds.), *A collection of papers.* The Hague: Mouton, 1970. Pp. 143–173.

Lakoff, George. Global rules. *Language,* 1970, **46**, 627–640. (b)

Lakoff, George. Instrumental adverbs and the concept of deep structure. *Foundations of Language,* 1968, **4**, 4–29.

Lakoff, George. *Irregularity in syntax.* New York: Holt, Rinehart & Winston, 1970. (c)

Lakoff, George. *Linguistics and natural logic.* Studies in generative semantics. Vol. 1. Ann Arbor: The University of Michigan Phonetics Laboratory, 1970. (d)

Lakoff, George. A note on ambiguity and vagueness. *Linguistic Inquiry,* 1970, **I**, 357–359. (a)

Lakoff, George. Some thoughts on transderivational constraints. Unpublished mimeo. University of Michigan, 1970. (c)

Lakoff, George. *Stative adjectives and verbs in English.* Report no. NSF-17 to the National Science Foundation. Cambridge, Mass.: Harvard University, The Computation Laboratory, 1966.

Lakoff, Robin T. *Abstract syntax and Latin complementation.* Research monograph no. 49. Cambridge, Mass.: M.I.T. Press, 1968.

Lakoff, Robin T. Some reasons why there can't be any *some–any* rule. *Language,* 1969, **45**, 608–616. (b)

Lakoff, Robin T. A syntactic argument for negative transportation. In Robert I. Binnick, Alice Davison, Georgia M. Green, and Jerry L. Morgan (Eds.), *Papers from the fifth regional meeting of the Chicago Linguistic Society.* Chicago: Univ. of Chicago Department of Linguistics, 1969. Pp. 140–148. (a)

Lakoff, Robin T. Tense and its relation to participants. *Language,* 1970, **46**, 838–850.

Lane, A. *A key to the art of letters.* London, 1700.

Langacker, Ronald W. 1969. On pronominalization and the chain of command. In David A. Reibel and Sanford A. Schane (Eds.), *Modern studies in English: Readings in transformational grammar.* Englewood Cliffs, N.J.: Prentice-Hall, 1969. Pp. 160–187.

Lee, Hong Bae, and Maxwell, Edward R. Performatives in Korean. In *Papers from the sixth regional meeting of the Chicago Linguistic Society.* Chicago: Chicago Linguistic Society, 1970. Pp. 363–380.

Lees, Robert B. A transformational grammar of English (reformulated). Unpublished ditto. University of Illinois, 1965.

Lees, Robert B., and Klima, Edward S. Rules for English pronominalization. *Language,* 1963, **39**, 17–28. Reprinted in David A. Reibel and Sanford A. Schane (Eds.), *Modern studies in English: Readings in transformational grammar.* Englewood Cliffs, N.J.: Prentice-Hall, 1969. Pp. 145–160.

McCawley, James D. English as a VSO language. *Language,* 1970, **46**, 286–300. (a)

McCawley, James D. Remarks on the lexicography of performative verbs. Paper presented at the 1973 conference on presuppositions, implicatures, and performances. Austin, Texas: University of Texas Press.

McCawley, James D. The role of semantics in a grammar. In Emmon Bach and Robert T. Harms (Eds.), *Universals in linguistic theory*. New York: Holt, Rinehart & Winston, 1968. Pp. 125–170.

McCawley, James D. Syntactic and logical arguments for semantic structure. In *Proceedings of the fifth international seminar on theoretical linguistics*. Tokyo: TEC Corp. To appear.

McCawley, James D. Tense and time references in English. In Charles Fillmore and D. Terence Langerdoen (Eds.), *Studies in linguistic semantics*. New York: Holt, Rinehart & Winston, 1971. Pp. 97–114.

McCawley, James D. Where do noun phrases come from? In Roderick A. Jacobs and Peter S. Rosenbaum (Eds.), *Readings in English transformational grammar*. Waltham, Mass.: Ginn, 1970. Pp. 166–183. (b)

Meillet, A. *Le Slave Commun*. Seconde Édition Revue et Augmentée avec le concours de A. Vaillant. Paris: Librairie Honoré Champion, 1965.

Morgan, Jerry L. On the treatment of presupposition in transformational grammar. In Robert I. Binnick, Alice Davison, Georgia M. Green, and Jerry L. Morgan (Eds.), *Papers from the fifth regional meeting of the Chicago Linguistic Society*. Chicago: Univ. of Chicago Department of Linguistics, 1969. Pp. 167–178.

Morgan, Jerry L. Sentence fragments and the notion "sentence." Unpublished mimeo. University of Illinois, 1972.

Newmeyer, Frederick J. The insertion of idioms. In Paul M. Peranteau, Judith N. Levi, and Gloria C. Phares (Eds.), *Papers from the eighth regional meeting of the Chicago Linguistic Society*. Chicago: Chicago Linguistic Society, 1972. Pp. 294–303.

Partee, Barbara Hall. Negation, conjunction and quantifiers: syntax vs. semantics. *Foundations of Language*, 1970, 6, 153–165.

Peranteau, Paul M., Levi, Judith N., and Phares, Gloria C. (Eds.). *Papers from the eighth regional meeting of the Chicago Linguistic Society*. Chicago: Chicago Linguistic Society, 1972.

Perlmutter, David. *Deep and surface constraints in syntax*. New York: Holt, Rinehart & Winston, 1972.

Postal, Paul M. On coreferent complement subject deletion. *Linguistic Inquiry*, 1970, I, 439–501. (b)

Postal, Paul M. A remark on the verb-initial hypothesis. *Papers in Linguistics*, 1972, 5, 124–138.

Postal, Paul M. On so-called "pronouns" in English. In Dineen (Ed.), *The 19th monograph on languages and linguistics*. Washington: Georgetown Univ. Press, 1966. Reprinted in David A. Reibel and Sanford A. Schane (Eds.), *Modern studies in English: Readings in transformational grammar*. Englewood Cliffs, N.J.: Prentice-Hall, 1969. Pp. 201–225.

Postal, Paul M. On the surface verb "remind." *Linguistic Inquiry*, 1970, I, 37–120. (a)

Quang, Phuc Dong. The applicability of transformations to idioms. In *Papers from the seventh regional meeting of the Chicago Linguistic Society*. Chicago: Chicago Linguistic Society, 1971. Pp. 198–206.

Reibel, David A., and Schane, Sanford A. (Eds.). *Modern studies in English: Readings in transformational grammar*. Englewood Cliffs, N.J.: Prentice-Hall, 1969.

Reichenbach, Hans. *Elements of symbolic logic*. New York: The Free Press, 1966.

Rosenbaum, Peter S. *The grammar of English predicate complement constructions*. Research monograph no. 47. Cambridge, Mass.: M.I.T. Press, 1967.

Ross, John Robert. Auxiliaries as main verbs. In William Todd (Ed.), *Studies in philosophical linguistics*, series one. Evanston, Ill.: Great Expectations, 1969. Pp. 77–102. (a)

Ross, John Robert. Constraints on variables in syntax. Unpublished Ph.D. dissertation. Massachusetts Institute of Technology, 1968. Reproduced by The Indiana University Linguistics Club, Bloomington, Ind.

Ross, John Robert. Guess who? In Robert I. Binnick, Alice Davison, Georgia M. Green, and Jerry L. Morgan (Eds.), *Papers from the fifth regional meeting of the Chicago Linguistic Society*. Chicago: Univ. of Chicago Department of Linguistics, 1969. Pp. 252–286. (b)

Ross, John Robert. On the cyclic nature of English pronominalization. In *To honor Roman Jakobson, II*. The Hague: Mouton, 1967. Pp. 1669–1682. Reprinted in David A. Reibel and Sanford A. Schane (Eds.), *Modern studies in English: Readings in transformational grammar*. Englewood Cliffs, N.J.: Prentice-Hall, 1969, Pp. 187–200.

Ross, John Robert. On declarative sentences. In Roderick A. Jacobs and Peter S. Rosenbaum (Eds.), *Readings in English transformational grammar*. Waltham, Mass.: Ginn, 1970. Pp. 222–272.

Ross, John Robert. Performatives from progressives? Unpublished ditto. Massachusetts Institute of Technology, 1969. (c)

Sadock, Jerrold. A conspiracy in Danish relative clause formation. In *The Chicago which hunt: Papers from the relative clause festival*. Pp. 59–63. Paravolume to Paul M. Peranteau, Judith N. Levi, and Gloria C. Phares (Eds.), *Papers from the eighth regional meeting of the Chicago Linguistic Society*. Chicago: Chicago Linguistic Society, 1972. (a)

Sadock, Jerrold M. Hypersentences. *Papers in Linguistics*, 1969, I, 283–371. (a)

Sadock, Jerrold M. A note on higher sentences. Unpublished paper. University of Illinois, 1967.

Sadock, Jerrold M. Queclaratives. In *Papers from the seventh regional meeting of the Chicago Linguistic Society*. Chicago: Chicago Linguistic Society, 1971. Pp. 223–232.

Sadock, Jerrold M. Speech act idioms. In Paul M. Peranteau, Judith N. Levi, and Gloria C. Phares (Eds.), *Papers from the eighth regional meeting of the Chicago Linguistic Society*. Chicago: Chicago Linguistic Society, 1972. Pp. 329–340. (b)

Sadock, Jerrold M., and Vanek, Anthony L. (Eds.). *Studies presented to Robert B. Lees by his students*. Edmonton, Canada: Linguistic Research, 1970.

Sadock, Jerrold M. Super-hypersentences. *Papers in Linguistics*, 1969, I, 1–16. (b)

Sadock, Jerrold M. Whimperatives. In Jerrold M. Sadock and Anthony L. Vanek (Eds.), *Studies presented to Robert B. Lees by his students*. Edmonton, Canada: Linguistic Research, 1970. Pp. 223–239.

Sampson, Geoffrey. *Nec plus supra*. Unpublished mimeo. Queen's College, Oxford, 1971.

Sapir, Edward. Male and female forms of speech in Yana. In David G. Mandelbaum (Ed.), *Selected writings of Edward Sapir in language, culture, and personality*. Berkeley: Univ. of California Press, 1958. Pp. 206–212.

Schreiber, Peter A. Style disjuncts and the performative analysis. *Linguistic Inquiry*, 1972, III, 321–348.

Schultz–Lorentzen. *Det Vestgrønlandske Sprog i grammatiske fremstilling. anden udgave, 2. oplag*. København: Ministeriet for Grønland, 1969.

Searle, John R. *Speech acts: an essay in the philosophy of language*. Cambridge, England: Cambridge Univ. Press, 1970.

Stockwell, Robert P., Schachter, Paul, and Partee, Barbara Hall *The major syntactic structures of English*. New York: Holt, Rinehart & Winston, 1973.

Strawson, P. F. Intention and convention in speech acts. *Philosophical Review*, 1964, **LXXII**, 439–460. Reprinted in J. R. Searle (Ed.), *The philosophy of language*. London: Oxford Univ. Press, 1971. Pp. 39–53.

Thorne, J. P. English imperative sentences. *Journal of Linguistics*, 1966, 2, 69–78.

Vendler, Zeno. *Res cogitans: An essay in rational psychology*. Ithaca: Cornell Univ. Press, 1972.

Weiser, Ann. *If you can imagine such a thing*. Unpublished M.A. paper. Univ. of Chicago, 1973.

Whitney, William D. *A compendious German grammar*. (5th ed., rev.) New York: Holt & Williams, 1870.

Zwicky, Arnold M. Auxiliary reduction in English. *Linguistic Inquiry*, 1970, 1, 320–323.

Zwicky, Arnold M. In a manner of speaking. *Linguistic Inquiry*, 1971, 2, 223–233.

Zwicky, Arnold M. Review of J. G. Kooij, *Ambiguity in natural language: An investigation of certain problems in its linguistic description*. Lingua. To appear.

Zwicky, Arnold M., and Sadock, Jerrold M. Failing the identity test (draft). Unpublished ditto. Ohio State University, 1973.

Zwicky, Arnold, and Zwicky, Ann D. *How come* and *what for*. In Braj B. Kachru, Robert B. Lees, Yakov Malkiel, Angelina R. Pietrangeli, and Sol Saporta (Eds.), *Issues in Linguistics: Papers in honor of Henry and Renée Kahane*. Urbana: Univ. of Illinois Press, 1973. Pp. 923–933.

Subject Index

165